Sparks of the Universe

At a time when the institutional Church is seeking a new vision for itself as the people of God, and when Catholic Schools are being encouraged to be more dialogical, more recontextualising and more hermeneutical, the universe gathers herself up and speaks. She does so in this new work of Jennifer Callanan, long respected as a leader and teacher of prayer which is open, inclusive, relevant and filled with the energy of a creation, holy and sacred. *Sparks of the Universe* invites us to feel the presence of God within and without ourselves; it holds out a challenge to us to be genuinely sacramental and to find and embrace the God who both creates and is created in our silence and contemplation. I commend this work to you: it models not only how we can pray, but how we can think of prayer, as the pervading and pervasive presence of divine love. It will enrich both those who lead and those who listen; teachers, catechists and lovers of the earth alike.

Dr Margaret Carswell,
Senior Lecturer, Faculty of Theology and Philosophy.
Australian Catholic University, Aquinas Campus, Ballarat, Victoria.

Sparks of the Universe is a fantastic resource for schools, staff and students to become more connected to the natural world through prayer and contemplation. The rituals enable staff to lead students in the skill of becoming truly still and noticing the presence of the sacred in themselves, each other and the surrounding environment. A wonderful resource to have in schools to continue the important work Pope Francis calls us to in becoming more aware of our common origins and being open to embracing an inner peace that connects us to each other and builds in us a deeper understanding of the interconnection of all creation through the sacred.

David Hillard,
Assistant Principal: Religious Identity and Mission.
St Margaret Mary's School, Croydon, South Australia.

Many schools and communities are engaged in the work of ecological conversion. It is work that connects children and young people with the mission of the church in a meaningful way. *Sparks of the Universe* draws on the wisdom of tradition and contemporary culture using language and ideas that are accessible for young people. The simplicity of the rituals makes this resource a great asset for bringing action to prayer and stillness.

Clare Nocka,
Principal.
St. Mary's Dominican R-12 College, Adelaide.

Pope Francis, in *Laudato Si'*, has called us all to a deeper appreciation and care for all creation. There are many ways we can deepen our care and respect for all that God has brought into being. In *Sparks of the Universe*, Jen Callanan has provided an exemplary series of rituals and reflections, that in age appropriate and contextually considered manner, invite school students and their teachers to draw on existing knowledge and skills to deepen their appreciation and love for creation.'

Rev. Dr Tony Densley,
Parish Priest.
Adelaide.

Rituals Awakening
Appreciation for Earth
our Common Home

Sparks of the Universe

Jennifer Callanan

COVENTRY
PRESS

Published in Australia by
Coventry Press
33 Scoresby Road
Bayswater Vic. 3153
Australia

ISBN 9780648725138

Copyright © Jennifer Callanan 2020

All rights reserved. Other than for the purposes and subject to the conditions prescribed under the *Copyright Act*, no part of this publication may be reproduced, stored in a retrieval system, or transmitted in any form or by any means, electronic, mechanical, photocopying, recording or otherwise, without the prior permission of the publisher.

Cataloguing-in-Publication entry is available from the National Library of Australia http://catalogue.nla.gov.au/.

Cover image: *Sparks of the Universe.* Original needle felting by Jennifer Callanan
Cover design by Ian James - www.jgd.com.au
Text design by Megan Low (FSG – Film Shot Graphics)

Typset in Merriweather size 10 on 14.5pts

Printed in Australia

Contents

Dedication 11
Acknowledgments 11
Foreword 12
Introduction 14
Using the Rituals 16
Further Possibilities 16
Creating a Sacred Space 16
Suggestion for Creating a Sacred Space on a Pinboard 16
Some Suggested Items in Readiness for Creating a Sacred Space 17
Beginning and Ending the School Day 17
Journal Writing 17

All the World is Sacred 19
All of Creation is Made of Star Dust 20
All the World is Sacred: a Listening Meditation 21
Bees are Amazing: Let's Celebrate! 22
Celebrating Our Pets 23
Celebrating St Francis of Assisi 24
Celebrating the Diversity of Mother Earth. A Litany 25
Celebrating the Extraordinary Golden Wattle 26
Creating a Nature Mandala 27
Listening to the Trees 28
Oceans are a Wonder 29
Place as Sacred: a Meditation 30
Walking Meditation 31
We Pray for the World 32
Whales: Singing One Song 33

Awakening to Mysteries of the Universe 35
Celebrating the Birth of the Universe 36
Deep Time Walk: a Walking History of Earth 38
Star Gazing: Contemplating the Night Sky 39
We are Made of Star Dust, Connected to All that Is: We are Grateful 40

Awareness of our Senses 41
Gratitude for our Five Senses 42
Gratitude for the Gift of Hearing 43
Gratitude for the Gift of Sight 44
Gratitude for the Gift of Smell 45
Gratitude for the Gift of Taste 46
Gratitude for the Gift of Touch 47
Mindfully Walking: Awakening the Senses 48
Noticing Nature 49

Beginnings, Endings and Times In-between 51
Beginning the Day 52
Celebrating the Conclusion of Primary School 53
Circle of Hope: Setting Intentions 54
Create a Circle of Hope: Reflecting on Our Intentions 55

    Concluding Secondary Schooling: Reflection and Blessing. 56
    Daily Gratitude 57
    End of Year Reflection 58
    Ending the Day. 59
    Greeting a New Day. 60
    Gratitude and Blessing for our Food 60
    Greeting the Darkness: as Day Turns to Night. 61
    Greeting the Light: as Night Turns to Day 62
    Pause, Reflect and Give Thanks for the Day 63
    Remembering the Day 64
    Welcoming Students to Primary School 65
    Welcoming Students to Secondary School 66

Called to Action 67
    Animals under Threat of Extinction: Creating a Mandala 68
    Celebrating What We Do to Make a Difference in the World 69
    Changing the Way We View Mother Earth. 70
    Earth Hour – Switch off – Connect to Earth 71
    Global School Climate Reflection 72
    My Choices Make a Difference: a Reflection 73
    Reflecting on our Daily Choices. Building up or Breaking down Mother Earth 74
    Random Acts of Kindness Make a Difference 75
    The World Can't Wait. A Message from Pope Francis 76
    The World is in Need of Healing. A Prayer of Lament 77
    We Lament Australian Animals under Threat of Extinction 78

Celebrating the Elements 79
    In Thanks for Air 80
    In Thanks for Fire 81
    In Thanks for Soil 82
    In Thanks for Water 83

Community Connection 85
    Celebrating Significant Women in our Lives 86
    Celebrating Significant Men in our Lives 87
    Environmental Sabbath – Earth Rest Day – A Litany 88
    National Schools Tree Day 89
    NAIDOC Week 90
    National Sorry Day 91
    National Sorry Day: A Lament. 92
    We Remember the World's Refugees with Encouragement, Support and Respect 93

Liturgical Moments 95
    Lent: A Time to Reflect on the Way We are Living our Lives 96
    Celebrating the Hope of Easter 97
    Creator Spirit: Ever Present 98
    Love is Born 99

Noticing the Seasons 101
    Noticing Autumn 102
    Autumn Equinox 103
    An Autumn Meditation: Creating a Mandala 104
    Noticing Winter 105
    Winter Solstice 106

Noticing Spring 107
Spring Equinox 108
Noticing Summer 109
Summer Solstice 110
Seasonal Fruits and Vegetables: Sparking the Imagination 111
Bibliography and Resources 112

Dedication

Desert Camels
Golden Wattle
Oscar Ned Edwards
Harriet Anne Wright
Black and White Swans
Ancient Rocks of the Great Ocean Road
New Holland Honeyeaters
Endangered Sea Turtles
Monarch Butterflies
Red and Molly
Night Skies
and all sparks of the universe, past, present and to come.

Acknowledgments

For editorial assistance: Ruth Bell, Dr Margaret Carswell, Dr Jenny Caruso, Rev. Dr Tony Densley, David Hillard and Mary Kelson.
For the Foreword: Gail Worcelo, gsm
For endorsements: Dr Margaret Carswell, Rev. Dr Tony Densley, David Hillard and Clare Nocka.
For photographs: 'Community Connection' and 'Awareness and Awakening to the Mysteries of the Universe', by Nicky Clark of *Macro to Infinity Photography*, used with permission. 'Noticing the Seasons', by Claire Taylor, used with permission. All other photographs by Jennifer Callanan.

Foreword

In his encyclical *Laudato Si'*, Pope Francis begins by saying he could not have written the encyclical without turning to that attractive and compelling figure, St Francis of Assisi, who holds a place of great influence and inspiration within the tradition of Christianity and throughout the world.

One of the most inspiring legends of St Francis of Assisi is the story of his encounter with the wolf of Gubbio, a ferocious wolf terrorising the village of Gubbio. The frightened townspeople complain to St Francis, asking him to deal with the situation.

According to the account, when the wolf of Gubbio sees St. Francis coming toward him, he runs forward, ready to attack. In response, St Francis raises his hand and makes the sign of the cross, immediately calming the wolf.

A conversation then begins between St Francis and the wolf, folding into the Catholic tradition a directive to all of us to learn how to *'listen to the voices of otherkind'*.

In the end, after careful listening and mutual sharing, St Francis and the wolf come to an agreement. The people of the town promise to bring food to the wolf regularly, leaving it on the outskirts of the village and the wolf agrees to cease frightening the townspeople so both wolf and human community can live in balance.

Jen Callanan's beautiful book of rituals, *Sparks of the Universe*, invites teachers and students, children and adults to 'listen to the voices of otherkind with whom we share our common home'.

The book design is as simple and gentle as the image of St Francis bending down to shake the paw of the wolf. The rituals are uncluttered yet poignant, focused and direct, inviting us to slow down and 'listen to the voices' of the natural world.

Fr Thomas Berry, the co-founder of our monastery (Green Mountain Monastery), wrote a short verse about children, entitled *It Takes a Universe*

The child awakens to a universe.
The mind of the child to a world of wonder.
Imagination to a world of beauty.
Emotion to a world of intimacy.
It takes a universe to make a child,
both in outer form and inner spirit.
It takes a universe to educate a child.
A universe to fulfil a child…

The simple rituals in *Sparks of the Universe* such as 'Star Gazing', 'World Day of Water', 'Place as Sacred' are designed to awaken the child and adult to a world of wonder, beauty and intimacy.

It is an honour to write the foreword to this book by Jen Callanan as she invites us into stillness so we can *'listen to the voices'* in this our common home.

May these rituals bring you and all you share them with into deeper intimacy with the community of life.

Gail Worcelo, sgm
Green Mountain Monastery and the Thomas Berry Sanctuary
Greensboro, Vermont USA

Image: 'St Francis Instructs the Wolf' by Carl Weidemeyer 1911
Sourced from: https://en.wikipedia.org/wiki/Wolf_of_Gubbio

Introduction

As a child, I grew up in Western Victoria, Australia, opposite Lake Colac. With my siblings and cousins, we spent hours exploring the lake bank, riding bikes into the bush, collecting mushrooms in local paddocks, and, of course, getting up to the occasional mischief. In the summer, we spent weeks at the beach exploring marine life in rock pools, swimming freely, oblivious to UV rays and generally connected with the natural world. We did not have words for our experiences; however, in hindsight, we were one with nature. We were engaged with our common home. In recent times, I have come to appreciate those amazing rock formations along the beaches of the Great Ocean Road, Victoria, and the extent to which our earth community has and continues to evolve.

In his encyclical, *Laudato Si'*, written in June 2015, Pope Francis urges all people of good will to engage with our common home, recognise our unity with all of creation and our moral and spiritual responsibility towards our shared environment. He is calling us all to awaken to our relationship with mother earth in these critical times. *Sparks of the Universe*, a book of rituals, is a contribution towards awakening our appreciation of our common home and shared origins with all of creation.

Because of our shared origins, it is no surprise that humans are healthier, more contented and creative when experiencing a connection with nature. David Attenborough tells us that 'No one will protect what they don't care about; and no one will care about what they have never experienced'. Connection is critical. These rituals invite connection and experience with nature.

Fr Thomas Berry (1999) reminds us that, 'For children to live only in contact with concrete and steel and wires and wheels and machines and computers and plastics, to seldom experience any primordial reality or even to see the stars at night, is a soul deprivation that diminishes the deepest of their human experience'. These rituals can reverently connect participants with the natural world.

In responding to the question, 'How can we speak about God?' the *Catechism of the Catholic Church* (1992) reminds us: 'We must (therefore) continually purify our language of everything in it that is limited, image-bound or imperfect, if we are not to confuse our image of God – "the inexpressible, the incomprehensible, the invisible, the ungraspable" – with our human representations. Our human words always fall short of the mystery of God.' [CCC:42]

Being aware of the limits of language, we are encouraged to expand our use of language in naming God. The Psalmist and Poets, and other Scripture authors are wonderful examples of doing this. The rituals in *Sparks of the Universe* reflect the intent of *Laudato Si'* in acknowledging an ever-present, pervasive God and uses many words in naming Divine Presence.

A candle lit at the beginning of a ritual can provide a focus and concrete metaphor, reminding us of the pervasive presence of Universal Sacredness, Divine Love, God, Great Mystery, Holy Spirit, Divine Energy.

The language used when lighting a candle reflects this understanding. For example:

'We light this candle. We acknowledge the presence of Divine Mystery in, with, and around us and all of creation.'

'As we light this candle, we are silent. We reverence Divine Presence.'

'We gather today. We are human expressions of Breath of Life.'

Sparks of the Universe rituals incorporate moments of silent contemplation. Silence can assist one's capacity to become present to the moment, increase inner calm and readiness for participation. Participants are simply invited to pause and be still.

The rituals are written with simplicity and focus. They are short and accessible with one per page and can be used with little or no preparation beyond what is written. Prayer facilitators use their own creativity in setting the scene and atmosphere for the rituals and adapt them as required, including adding reflective music and songs.

I thank Gail Worcelo, sgm, for writing the Foreword; Margaret Carswell, Tony Densley and David Hillard for their endorsements and editorial assistance; Clare Nocka for her endorsement; Mary Kelson for editorial assistance; Nicky Clark, of 'Macro to Infinity Photography' for the use of three of her images; Michelle Abbott, Ruth Bell, and David Hillard who trialled several rituals and provided valuable feedback and many others who assisted along the way.

Margie Abbott invited me to write a book of rituals together. It became evident that our audiences were different and from there emerged Margie's book entitled *Cosmic Sparks* orientated towards adults and spiritual seekers and this book, *Sparks of the Universe,* orientated to young people and adolescents embracing a spirit of *Laudato Si'* and Ecological Conversion. I am grateful for Margie's passion and companioning throughout the writing process and the birth of these books.

Let us all further recognise our unity with creation, our moral and spiritual responsibility towards creation, and our capacity to celebrate the diverse sparks of the universe.

Jennifer Callanan
jennifermarycallanan@gmail.com

Using the Rituals

As mentioned in the introduction, the rituals are written with simplicity and focus. They are short and accessible with one per page and can be used with little or no preparation beyond what is written. Prayer facilitators use their own creativity in setting the scene and atmosphere for the rituals and adapt them as required, including added reflective music and songs.

Young people and adults alike can prepare and lead the rituals. Young people will grow in confidence and capacity as they take leadership and recognise what is possible. The rituals can be used as models and adapted for future celebrations suited to your setting.

Further Possibilities

Several of the rituals have suggested ways to integrate the ritual into the wider context of your setting. Some of these suggestions involve activities as preparation prior to the celebration or as a follow up at the conclusion.

Creating a Sacred Space

When a Sacred Space is created, the mood and intent of the current space changes in readiness for prayer or ritual. Sacred Spaces can be permanent or temporary. Within the school setting, often a Sacred Space is created in preparation for prayer or liturgy, transforming a large hall, classroom or outside space setting for the anticipated ritual. At times, the Sacred Space will be set prior to people gathering. At other times the Sacred Space will be created by those gathered, integral to the ritual itself.

Many classrooms have permanent Sacred Spaces. A permanent Sacred Space on a pinboard where it is visible by all may be suitable. A temporary Sacred Space can then be created for prayer and ritual occasions.

Suggestion for Creating a Sacred Space on a Pinboard

Choose a large image of Mother Earth or the Universe.
Place this on an appropriate noticeboard, preferably up the front where it will be noticed.
Surround the image with a range of metaphors for the greatest of all mysteries. For example: Great Mystery, Creative Energy, Breath of Life, God, Creator Spirit, Divine Love.
Surround the outer circle of the image with reflective prayer starters. For example: Blessed be..., I am Grateful..., I Wonder..., Today I ...,

This visual, or similar, can assist the students when leading spontaneous prayer using the following process:

    A minute of silence.
    The leader begins, using one of the phrases around the image.
    For example:
    'I am grateful for all the opportunities ahead of me today. I am grateful.'
    Other students are invited to contribute.
    At the conclusion, the leader simply says, 'We are grateful', and all respond, 'We are grateful.'

Some Suggested Items in Readiness for Creating a Sacred Space

Candles, coloured cloths and ribbons.
A collection of natural objects, for example stones, shells, autumn leaves, fruit, vegetables and flowers.
Images of various scenes and themes including: the universe, people, stars, planets, vegetation, animal life, the ocean, multi-cultural communities, seasons, birds, and more.
Contemporary religious images. A globe or map of the world. Small bell or chime. Glass beads.

Beginning and Ending the School Day

In my experience, the morning classroom/homeroom gathering in a primary and secondary setting can often be taken up with notices, students getting organised for the day and general rushing within a short period of time. Anticipation looms. A sense of 'getting on with the day' is ever present. Students come into the classroom carrying various experiences, some processed and others sitting heavily within them. In the busyness at the end of the day when everyone is 'done' and wants to get on with the next thing, there is a sense of urgency to 'get out' of the classroom, push forward and let go of what has been.

The Beginning and Ending of the Day are transition moments for both teachers and students. This transition provides an opportunity for reflection, making meaning and readiness for the next moment.

The Class Teacher or Home Room Teacher can create a reflective structure, for 2-3 minutes, within their morning and end of the day practices. This structure may assist the students develop skills of reflective contemplation, creating a space and readiness for their transition from what has been to what is coming. Built into the structure of the day, students will anticipate this time as the 'norm' and grow in their capacity for quiet stillness, contemplation and meditation.

The capacity to be still grows slowly and within a variety of moments and experiences. Our role as educators is to create these moments.

Journal Writing

Occasionally, rituals lend themselves for participants to record their reflections in their journal. Writing thoughts, feelings, experiences, questions, hopes and dreams can assist in understanding them more clearly. Ideas can be generated, insights gained, and thoughts clarified. It is important that participants are aware that no one else is privy to their writings unless, of course, they chose to share them.

All the World is Sacred

All of Creation is Made of Star Dust

Leader: We gather in silence knowing that all of creation is made of star dust.

Pause for one minute.

Leader: The earth came forth from the Great Flaring Forth 13.7 billion years ago.

Reader 1: All people, creatures and the natural world in Australia are made of star dust!
Mother, we hear your heartbeat.
All: Mother, we hear your heartbeat.

Reader 2: All people, creatures and the natural world in Asia are made of star dust!
Mother, we hear your heartbeat.
All: Mother, we hear your heartbeat.

Reader 3: All people, creatures and the natural world in North America are made of star dust.
Mother, we hear your heartbeat.
All: Mother, we hear your heartbeat.

Reader 4: All people, creatures and the natural world in South America are made of star dust.
Mother, we hear your heartbeat.
All: Mother, we hear your heartbeat.

Reader 5: All people, creatures and the natural world in Europe are made of star dust.
Mother, we hear your heartbeat.
All: Mother, we hear your heartbeat.

Reader 6: All people, creatures and the natural world in Antarctica are made of star dust.
Mother, we hear your heartbeat.
All: Mother, we hear your heartbeat.

Reader 7: All people, creatures and the natural world in Africa are made of star dust.
Mother, we hear your heartbeat.
All: Mother, we hear your heartbeat.

An opportunity for participants to name a place they wish to remember.

Reader: All people, creatures and the natural world in … are made of stardust.
Mother, we hear your heartbeat.
All: Mother, we hear your heartbeat.

Leader: Yes, we remember today that all of creation is made of star dust.
All: Yes, we remember today that all of creation is made of star dust.

Acknowledgment: Response inspired by the song, 'Mother I Feel You' by Windsong Dianne Martin on the CDs titled, 'Love is the Medicine' and 'Mother I Feel You.' Downloadable from website: http://www.windsongmakani.com/

All the World is Sacred: a Listening Meditation

Song by Peter Kearney. Used with permission.

Leader: Settle yourself into a comfortable position. Relax and focus on your breathing. Today we will experience simply listening to the song, 'All the World is Sacred'. Images and thoughts might come into your mind about your own special places in nature. Let the images come and go as you listen.

Play the song.

All the world is sacred in my eyes.
All the world is sacred in my eyes.
This world is holy.
This world is holy, hallelujah, surely,
All the world is sacred in my eyes.

Every tree, God's beauty dressed in green.
In the creeks and mountains, God is seen.
In the great gum gully, in seagulls soaring, thunder roaring, surely,
All the world is sacred in my eyes.

God creates all life; this world is good.
Earth is in our care and care we should.
She is our mother,
So be careful, sister, brother, surely,
All the world is sacred in my eyes.

If we can just hear with hearts amazed.
Every stone is singing songs of praise.
This world is holy.
This world is holy, hallelujah, surely,
All the world is sacred in my eyes.

All the world is sacred in my eyes.
All the world is sacred in my eyes.
This world is holy.
This world is holy, hallelujah, surely,
All the world is sacred in my eyes.

All the world is sacred in my eyes.
All the world is sacred in my eyes.

Pause

Leader: Yes! All the world is sacred. Amen.
All: Yes! All the world is sacred. Amen.

Further Possibilities
*'All the World is Sacred' (Track 2) can be auditioned and downloaded from the following site: https://store.cdbaby.com/cd/peterkearney5
*The song can be used as a meditation, at the beginning or conclusion of a ritual, or as a meditation leading to artistic expression. Acknowledge author each time it is used. Peter Kearney Website, with further works by Peter: http://www.peterkearneysongs.com.au/

All the World is Sacred

Bees are Amazing: Let's Celebrate!

World Bee Day is celebrated May 20th; however can be celebrated at any time.
This day acknowledges bees and other pollinators for their critical role in the ecosystem.

Leader: We gather today celebrating the amazing role of bees in the ecosystem.
As you come to stillness, notice your breathing. Notice when your in breath becomes your out breath and when your out breath becomes your in breath.

Pause

We light this candle, acknowledging that each one gathered reflects the wonder of Divine Mystery. And yes, we acknowledge that each creature, including bees, reflects the face of God.

Reader 1: We celebrate over 20,000 different types of bees in the world.
All: Blessed be the bees.

Reader 2: Among the many insects that pollinate plants, bees play the most crucial role.
All: Blessed be the bees.

Reader 3: Pollination is important because it leads to the production of fruits and vegetables that can be eaten and seeds that will create more plants.
All: Blessed be the bees.

Reader 4: Pope Francis reminds us that each creature reflects the face of God and that all of creation is interconnected. [LS:221]

Reader 5: We know many pesticides are harmful to bees and we are aware that bees around the world are under great threat. We lament the mistreatment of bees.

Pause

Reader 6: Bees have been declared the most important being on earth.

Pause

Leader: We give thanks for bees and their remarkable role as pollinators in the biodiversity of plant life. We give thanks for bees.
All: We give thanks for bees.

Further Possibilities
*Images of bees could be prepared ready to be placed around the candle during the ritual.
*Prior to the ritual, the group make Honey Joys, using honey and corn flakes. Google a recipe. At the conclusion, participants share the Honey Joys celebrating the gift of honey from bees. They could also invite a younger class to share in the ritual.
*Students research the process of pollination and local bee-attracting plants.
*This ritual could be used as a model. Students are assigned or choose a creature. In pairs, they research facts and create a ritual. A book of rituals is then created for further use with the group and/or shared with other classes.

Celebrating Our Pets

Participants bring a photo of their pets.

Leader: As we light this candle, we remember we are in universal kinship with all of creation. Pope Francis reminds that we see God reflected in all that exists, [LS:87] and yes, that means our pets!

As you sit around the circle, focus on the central candle and gently settle into this space.

Today, we celebrate and give thanks for the various pets we have adopted and care for.
Sadly too, we remember that many animals are treated cruelly in homes and for the sake of profit.

Pause

Leader: St Francis of Assisi recognised that all of creation is filled with Divine Love and he had special love for animals and called them his brothers and sisters.

We bring our pets here, in our sacred circle, acknowledging their unique spark of Divine Love.

We sit for a moment in silence.

Let's begin, one at a time. Introduce your pet, their name and what you notice and appreciate about them.

When you finish, place the image of your pet around the candle and say, Blessed be_____ (*insert the name of your pet.*)

When circle is completed:

Leader: Raise your right hand in a gesture of blessing and repeat after me.
    We bless pets for their loyalty and unconditional love.
    We bless the uniqueness and variety of each pet.
    We bless the many people who work towards care for all animals.
    Blessed be pets. Amen.
All: Blessed be pets. Amen.

At the conclusion of the ritual, the images can be displayed on a notice board with their names and other information.

Further Possibilities
*Research animal welfare activists around the world and bring their names and work to the ritual.
*Acknowledge that many animals are treated cruelly. Create a ritual of lament.

All the World is Sacred

Celebrating St Francis of Assisi
Feast Day October 4th.

Leader: As we gather to celebrate the feast St Francis of Assisi, relax your body.
Take a long deep breath in and then a long breath out. Repeat three times.
Now allow your breath to return to its natural rhythm. One breath after another.

Reader 1: We light the central candle, remembering that St Francis saw the world in universal kinship. He saw the moon, water, mother earth and birds as sisters; and the sun, wind, fire and creatures as his brothers. Yes, we are one with all of creation.
All: Yes, we are one with all of creation.

Reader 2: St Francis recognised that all of creation is filled with Divine Love.

Reader 3: St Francis was gentle in caring for earth and all creatures.

Reader 4: St Francis was committed to living simply, using only what he needed.

Reader 5: St Francis saw beauty and brightness in all of creation.

Reader 4: St Francis spent time in silence and prayer.

Reader 6: St Francis followed his heart and his love for God, present everywhere.

Reader 7: St Francis recognised every aspect of creation, and yes, each of us, as an outpouring of Divine Love. He reminds us that we belong to one universal family.

Leader: We now read together a prayer of peace inspired by St Francis.

Left Side:
    We have the capacity to be instruments of peace.
    Where there is sadness in others, we show love and care.
    Where there is doubt and confusion amongst our friends, we listen and ask questions.
    Where there is exclusion, we have courage to welcome.
    Where there is disregard for the environment, we speak up and act.
    Where there is disrespect for animals, we show compassion and care.

Right Side:
    We are instruments of peace when we are gentle and care for earth and all creatures.
    We are instrument of peace when we pause and notice the night sky.
    We are instruments of peace when we take a moment before we respond.
    We are instruments of peace when we speak out against cruelty to animals.
    We are instrument of peace when we take time to be silent.
    We are instruments of peace. Amen.
All: Amen.

Further Possibilities
*Print a copy of the ritual for participants.
*Many school libraries have stories of St Francis. Choose one to read at the beginning or during the ritual.
*Students can create their own peace prayer using the above as a model and a class collection can be created.

Celebrating the Diversity of Mother Earth.
A Litany

Leader: Today we come together in blessing for the diversity of Mother Earth.
We begin with a moment of silence.

In your silence, with eyes closed, think of your favourite place on earth. It might be a beach, a park, a special river, or a tree. Imagine yourself there and listen to the sounds, notice the colours, recall the smells, observe what is happening.

Pause

Reader 1:	Blessed be the diversity of Mother Earth.
All:	Blessed be the diversity of Mother Earth.
Reader 2:	Blessed be trees, creating homes, standing tall, giving shade and produce.
All:	Blessed be the diversity of Mother Earth.
Reader 3:	Blessed be rivers, flowing and sustaining life.
All:	Blessed be the diversity of Mother Earth.
Reader 4:	Blessed be the sea and all the extraordinary creatures living there.
All:	Blessed be the diversity of Mother Earth.
Reader 5:	Blessed be vegetation and the amazing variety of colours, shapes and sizes of flowers, fruits and vegetables.
All:	Blessed be the diversity of Mother Earth.
Reader 6:	Blessed be animals, from the tiniest of insects to the largest of blue whales.
All:	Blessed be the diversity of Mother Earth.
Reader 7:	Blessed be all people of the world with their unique spark of love and capacity to enjoy and care for Mother Earth and all her creatures.
All:	Blessed be the diversity of Mother Earth.
Leader:	Think of some ways that you will care for Mother Earth today, tomorrow and in the future.
	Invite 3-4 participants to respond.
Leader:	We give thanks for the diversity of Mother Earth. Amen.
All:	Amen.

Further Possibilities
*Collect images beforehand to match each phrase. These are then placed around the candle as the phrase is read.
*Students could use this model to create their own litany and create a booklet using the phrases, responses and appropriate pictures. These booklets could be shared with other classes or kept in the class prayer collection.

All the World is Sacred

Celebrating the Extraordinary Golden Wattle

Wattle Day is celebrated in Australia on September 1st, the official start of Australian Spring.
This ritual is best celebrated outside.

Leader: Today, we celebrate Australia's national floral emblem, the Golden Wattle.

Reader 1: As we begin our Wattle Day celebration, we acknowledge the Traditional Custodians of the land on which we gather, the _____ People. *(add in the name of the local Indigenous group)*. We recognise their continuing connection to land and community. We pay respects to Elders past, present and emerging.
Green and gold cloths are a placed around the central candle. A piece of wattle is place on the cloths.

Leader: Let us pause in silence for a few moments. We acknowledge the presence of Divine Mystery in, with and around us as we gather to celebrate the extraordinary Golden Wattle.

Reader 2: Acacia pycnantha, most commonly known as the Golden Wattle, is native to south-eastern Australia, and blooms in spring.
All: We give thanks for Golden Wattle.

Reader 3: Wattle is ideally suited to withstand Australia's droughts, winds and bushfires. Some say the resilience of wattle represents the spirit of Australian people.
All: We give thanks for Golden Wattle.

Reader 4: Wattle grows to a height of 8 metres and has phyllodes, flattened leaf stalks, instead of true leaves.
All: We give thanks for Golden Wattle.

Leader: Pope Francis reminds us that everything is interconnected and urges us to learn about the diversity of creation. We are part of nature and constantly interact with it. [LS:138, 139]

Reader 5: There are more than 1,350 wattle species in the world; Australia has almost 1,000.
All: We give thanks for extraordinary diversity.

Reader 6: The tannin rich inner bark and gums of wattles have healing effects, and this has been known by First Nations People for thousands of years.
All: We give thanks for wise knowing.

Reader 7: Wattle seeds are very nutritious and can be used to make a type of flour. They can also be dark roasted and used to make a drink or added to chocolate or desserts.
All: We give thanks for wattle seeds.

Reader 8: Parts of the young flowers, and leaves stepped in water, can be consumed. The leaves can also be used for weaving. We give thanks for the generous Golden Wattle. Amen.
All: We give thanks for the generous Golden Wattle. Amen.

Further Possibilities
*Collect sprigs of wattle for sharing during the ritual. As each statement is read, a sprig of wattle is placed around the candle.
*Plan a walk around the local neighbourhood looking out for wattle trees.
*Purchase small tubes of several wattle varieties and after the ritual plant them in the school grounds with identifying plaques.
*Participants could create rituals related to the floral emblem of a country of their choice using the above as a model. These rituals could be collected and created into a book.

Creating a Nature Mandala

Creating a nature mandala is an opportunity to work with natural materials while experiencing a meditation.

Gather in a suitable outdoor space where there are natural materials on the ground. For example, at the beach, camp or retreat bush setting.

Leader: *Inquire from the group what they know about mandalas. You can use information below, a prepared PowerPoint or printed images of nature mandalas when introducing to the group.*

The word mandala comes from the Sanskrit meaning 'circle'. The mandala is one of humankind's most ancient art forms. Various types of mandalas may be found in several religions, cultural art forms and in architecture. In churches, we often find stunning mandalas in the form of a rose window, a circular, stained-glass design symbolising many stories. A mandala is generally circular with symmetrical features, often telling a story in images or symbols or simply a creative expression of the moment.

Leader: Pope Francis tells us that nature is a constant source of awe and wonder. [LS:85]
Today, we have an opportunity to create a mandala using natural materials only.
These natural materials will be found on the ground, which means we won't be pulling leaves from trees or using other items. Each mandala created will have its own beauty and uniqueness and remember creating a mandala is not a competition – it is simply the unique creation of the individual or group.
You will have time to create your nature mandala either alone, or in groups of no more than four. We will gather together at the conclusion of our time.

Instruct the group about the location parameters for creating their mandala and suggested diameter limit. Participants are free to chat during their creating while respecting others around them.

Enjoy experiencing your mandala unfold.

Conclusion.
Invite the students to walk around in silence appreciating the various mandalas created by their colleagues, peers, friends.

Gather the group together. Allow for sharing of experiences.

Leader: We honour Creative Energy flowing uniquely through each of us today. Amen.
All: We honour Creative Energy. Amen.

The mandalas remain on the ground and will eventually return to the earth.

Further Possibilities
*Google and gather several images of mandalas to create a PowerPoint. You will find many nature mandalas to include. Use these images at the beginning of the ritual together with a shared understanding of mandalas.

All the World is Sacred

Listening to the Trees

A ritual for celebration within the school grounds, camp, reflection day
or other suitable place where there are trees.

Gather around a large tree in a circle or semi-circle.

Leader: As we gather, feel your feet on the ground. Gradually come to stillness and become aware of your breathing.

Reader 1: We acknowledge the Traditional Custodians of the land on which we gather, the _____ People. *(Add in the name of local Indigenous group.)* We recognise their continuing connection to land and community. We pay respects to Elders past, present and emerging.

Leader: As we stand around this _____ tree, we remember that Pope Francis reminds us that the entire universe speaks of God's love. Soil, water, mountains, trees: everything is a touch of God. [LS:84]
Notice the sounds around you and any movement in the air.
Notice the leaves, the branches, the colour and shape of this tree.

Pause for a few moments. You might invite participants to share what they notice.

Leader: I wonder what messages this tree might have for us today.

Reader 2: *Step forward and stand by the tree.*
Like you, I have evolved from the primordial Flaring Forth and carry within me sparks of the universe.

Reader 3: *Step forward and stand by the tree.*
Like you, I require sunshine, rain, nourishment and the right conditions to prosper and grow.

Reader 4: *Step forward and stand by the tree.*
Like you, I grow exactly where I am, simply being myself.

Reader 5: *Step forward and stand by the tree.*
Like you, I prefer not to be alone and I welcome the company of other trees.

Reader 6: *Step forward and stand by the tree.*
Like you, I need strong roots and support when the winds blow, and things get tough.

Reader 7: *Step forward and stand by the tree.*
I lament that many trees are destroyed in the name of profit.
   Pause with head down.
I lament that many animals lose their habitat when trees are cut down.
   Pause with head down.
I lament that many people are unaware of the amazing role trees play in keeping the air supply clean.
   Pause with head down.

Leader: We have listened, and we are in awe of this tree, and all trees.
We give thanks for trees. Amen.
All: We give thanks trees. Amen.

Further Possibilities
*Participants choose a plant and create a ritual modelled on the above. These rituals could be gathered and created into a class book and gifted to other classes.

All the World is Sacred

Oceans are a Wonder

This ritual could be celebrated on the beach, in the classroom, oval or other suitable space.

Leader: We sit in our sacred circle, mindful of earth's oceans.
Yes, oceans are a wonder.

Make yourself comfortable and become aware of your breathing. Notice the gentle rhythm of your breath.

Reader 1: We light the candle in awe of Divine Mystery present and active here and within all oceans of the world.

Reader 2: Earth's oceans are a world of mystery, magic and beauty. From fascinating marine life to waters themselves. There is so much to discover about the ocean.

Reader 3: 3.8 billion years ago, the earth's temperature cooled, allowing water to condense from gas into rain.

Reader 4: 3 billion years ago, life on earth was restricted to oceans during evolution.

Reader 5: 70% of the earth's surface is covered by ocean.

Reader 6: 90% of an iceberg is submerged below the water's surface.

Reader 7: Blue oceans: water absorbs red light of the colour spectrum, leaving the blue for us to see.

Reader 8: 3,700 metres is the average depth of the ocean.

Reader 9: 50 times more carbon is held in the ocean than in the atmosphere.

Reader 10: 28 major groups of animals live in the ocean, whereas only 11 live on land.

Reader 11: 33 metres is the length of the largest recorded blue whale.

Reader 12: The world's tallest mountain is found in the Pacific Ocean known as Mauna Kea, 10 kms high. Mt Everest is 8.8kms.

Leader: Yes, oceans are a wonder. Amen.
All: Yes, oceans are a wonder. Amen.

Reference: https://www.divein.com/articles/ocean-facts/

Further Possibilities
*Prior to the ritual, participants gather facts about the ocean and share these during the ritual.
*A globe of the world is placed in the centre beside the candle.
*Names of the world's oceans printed and placed around the central space.

Place as Sacred: a Meditation

Pope Francis tells us that, 'Soil, water, mountains: yes everything, as it were, is a caress of God. The history of our friendship with God is always linked to places which take on an intensely personal meaning; we all remember places, revisiting those memories does us much good. Anyone who has grown up in the hills or used to sit by the spring to drink or played outdoors in the neighbourhood; going back to these places is a chance to recover something of their true selves.' [LS:84]

Leader: Many of us have special places we visit with family, friends or alone. It might be camping in the bush, surfing at a favourite spot, walking along the beach, visiting a favourite National Park, fishing by a river and much more.

Pope Francis reminds us that soil, water, mountains – everything is a touch of God.

During our meditation today, you will take some time to reflect on your favourite place in nature.

Make yourself comfortable. Sitting or lying down, eyes open or closed. Whatever works best for you. Become aware of your breathing. Gently notice the in breath and when it becomes the out breath. Focus on the natural rhythm of your breathing.

Leader: Think of a place that makes you come alive, a place in nature that you really like.

Visualise this place and notice what is around you.

Imagine the familiar sounds.

Notice how you are feeling when you remember this place.

Are you alone or are others with you?

Take a few moments to remember why this place is special to you.

Pause

Leader: Pope Francis reminds us that all of creation continues to reveal a unique spark of Divine Love.
Our special places reveal something of God to each of us.
We are thankful.
All: We are thankful.

Further possibilities
*Prior to the ritual, participants could be given time to gather some images of their favourite places in nature and share these during the ritual.
*Create a display board naming natural wonders, national parks, and other sacred sites.

All the World is Sacred

Walking Meditation

This ritual can be experience at school, during retreats, at camp and other suitable times.
Gather outside, on soft dry grass or the beach.

Leader: Today, we will take part in a walking meditation. It is best if you take off your shoes.

Pause

Leader: Let us stand in our circle in silence for one minute.
Become aware of your breath. In and out. In and out.
Become aware of Creative, Divine Presence in, with and around you.

Pause

Leader: Feel your feet on the ground.
As you stand, become aware of the great fireball in the centre of the earth.

Pause.

Leader: Focus now on the earth's surface you are standing on today.

Pause

Leader: Notice what you are feeling under your feet.
Is it soft, hard, rough, smooth, bumpy?

Pause

Leader: Repeat after me.
Mother Earth, I feel you on the soles of my feet.
All: Mother Earth, I feel you on the soles of my feet.

Leader: Now, take one step back and stand tall still paying attention to the soles of your feet connecting with Mother Earth.

Pause

Leader: Now turn around facing out of the circle. Wander around in silence. After every 5 steps, pause and say to yourself: Mother Earth, I feel you on the soles of my feet. After about 10-15 minutes, make your way in back to the circle.

When all have gathered, pause in silence for one minute.

Leader: Together we say: Mother Earth, we feel you on the soles of our feet.
All: Mother Earth, we feel you on the soles of our feet.

Acknowledgment: Meditation inspired by the song, 'Mother I Feel You.' by Windsong Dianne Martin on the CDs titled, 'Love is the Medicine' and 'Mother I Feel You.' Downloadable from website: http://www.windsongmakani.com/

All the World is Sacred

We Pray for the World

Leader:	We gather around our candle, mindful of Divine Presence in, with and around us. Take a few moments to become comfortable and still. Let your mind focus on our amazing world. *Pause* We dream of a world where all the people care for each other, are happy and live in harmony with creation.
All:	We dream.
Side A:	We notice the natural environment; and that many creatures and gifts of the earth are not always treated with respect.
All:	We notice.
Side B:	We are mindful that many people are forced to leave their home country with nowhere to go.
All:	We are mindful.
Side A:	We lament that people die because of war, terrorism, homelessness and hunger.
All:	We lament.
Side B:	We are aware that sometimes we hurt each other with the things we say and do and the things we don't do.
All:	We are aware.
Leader:	*Invite participants to add their own prayer.* *Pause*
Side A:	We remember our world is for all people to feel safe and happy and to belong.
All:	We remember.
Side B:	We remember that everything in the world is to be shared equally for all.
All:	We remember.
Side A:	We remember to be kind, friendly and encouraging with each other.
All:	We remember.
Side B:	We remember that we are one with mother earth and we are responsible to care for her and all her creatures.
All:	We remember.
Leader:	Invite anyone who wishes to add their own: 'We remember…'
Leader:	Our world is a wonderful place. We dream that our world leaders will make decisions showing that all inhabitants are precious. Like Jesus, may we remember to make choices that show love, justice, care for each other and the world. Amen.
All:	Amen.

Further Possibilities
*A globe of the world placed in the centre of the circle with various images of people, creation, and creatures scattered around.

All the World is Sacred

Whales: Singing One Song

Leader: Today, we gather in our circle to honour and appreciate our brother and sister whales. Become aware of your body as you settle into this space. Notice the rhythm of your breathing.
Pause for a few moments.

Reader 1: We light the central candle remembering Pope Francis and his message in Laudato Si'. We are bonded with all creatures as brothers and sisters, all permeated with Divine Love. [LS:92]
Pause
Reader 2: The ancient song of whales has circled the globe for millions of years, a song that continues to change and evolve, and sung in unison by all within a thousand kilometres sometimes lasting up to 24 hours. Imagine that!
All: Blessed be whales.
Pause
Reader 3: It is thought that a whale's song unimpeded, could circle the globe and return to its sender. A great underwater chorus weaving a sonic web of positive frequency throughout the waters of planet earth. Imagine that!
Pause
Reader 4: With thousands of whales moving along ancient migration trails each year, some believe that their song lines not only help them navigate, communicate, and swoon their mates, but also help keep the magnetic fields of planet earth in balance. Imagine that!
All: Blessed be whales.
Pause
Reader 5: Whales are fundamentally integral to the biological balance of the oceans and therefore planet earth. Imagine that!
All: Blessed be whales.
Pause
Reader 6: Whales continual passage from the dark depths of the ocean up to the surface layer that receives sunlight and back down again, triggers the vital life cycle of oxygen producing plankton. Plankton in turn absorb vast amounts of carbon dioxide from the atmosphere drawing it back to the ocean depths each year. Imagine that!
All: Blessed be whales.
Pause
Reader 7: As much as the whales need us, we need the whales for the critical, balancing role they play in the oceans and for their powerful reminder that it really is possible to sing one song together. Blessed be whales.
All: Blessed be whales.
Pause
Reader 8: Whales have lived in harmony in earth's oceans for over 50 million years. Blessed be whales.
All: Blessed be whales.
Pause
Leader: Yes, we give thanks for whales who call us to remember to rise as one family and realise how powerful we are when we come together in peace for the greater good of all. Blessed be whales.
All: Blessed be whales.

Reference: Words drawn and adapted from Chip Richard's article, 'The Healing Power of the Whales' Song.' Used with permission. Cited here: https://upliftconnect.com/healing-power-whales-song/ Further Information: www.chiprichards.global

Further Possibilities
*Images of whales are collected and placed around the sacred space after each phrase.
*Prior to the ritual, view 'How Whales Change Climate' https://www.youtube.com/watch?v=M18HxXve3CM#action=share
*Participants investigate cruelty and disrespect for whales around the world and create a litany of lament.

Awakening to Mysteries of the Universe

Awakening to Mysteries of the Universe

Celebrating the Birth of the Universe

'The Cosmic Walk' is a ritual created by Dominican Sr Miriam Therese MacGillis of Genesis Farm, New Jersey. It has been modified and facilitated by many people around the world. The Cosmic Walk is a way of bringing our knowledge of the 14-billion-year Universe process from our heads to our hearts. This ritual is best celebrated outside, ideally using a large rope to create a spiral with unlit candles at various points to acknowledge moments of creation. The ritual can also be celebrated inside. A large candle is in the centre of the spiral. After each phrase is read, a participant walks forward and lights the next candle.

Leader: Today we gather to celebrate the birth of the universe some 13.7 billion years ago. As we stand in silence, we acknowledge the Traditional Custodians of the land on which we gather, the _____ People.

We gather in awe of the mysteries of the universe and reverence Divine Presence.
Pause.

Reader 1: In the beginning Great Mystery is present in silence. *The central candle is lit.*

Reader 2: 13.7 billion years ago, there is a great flaring forth, a great fire ball, a great outpouring of Divine Energy and the universe story begins.

Reader 3: After nearly a billion years the universe cools, atoms form, and hydrogen and helium fills the expanding space and stars are born.

Reader 4: 4.6 billion years ago, a Grandmother Star becomes a supernova giving rise to a star, the Sun.

Reader 5: 4.5 billion years ago, the solar system forms from the remains of the supernova explosion. A Mars size body impacts the Earth. The Moon is born and earth tilts 23 degrees to the side, giving birth to the seasons of the year.

Reader 6: 4.4 - 4.1 billion years ago, the earth surface cools and the first rain falls.

Reader 7: 4 billion years ago, the first cells emerge and begin to divide.

Reader 8: 3.9 billion years ago, small creatures learn to capture the sun and store energy.

Reader 9: 2.7 billion years ago, oxygen-loving cells emerge. Oxygen levels continue to rise until they reach near present-day levels.

Reader 10: 2 billion years ago, the earth is spinning fast and one day is 18 hours.

Reader 11: 1.5 billion years ago, sexual union arises where previous reproduction was with cells growing and dividing.

Reader 12: 700 million years ago, some organisms begin to live in colonies. Community is born.

Reader 13: 600 million years ago, light sensitive eyespots evolve into eyesight. The first animals to evolve in the ocean are soft bodied.

Reader 14: 460 million years ago, animals leave the water, worms, molluscs and crustaceans. Algae, fungi and insects evolve.

Reader 15: 395 million years ago, frogs and toads evolve and emerge from the water.

Reader 16: 335 million years ago, forests evolve, and the great age of reptiles begins.

Reader 17: 235 million years ago, the 4th mass extinction takes place, ancestors of dinosaurs emerge.

Reader 18: 225 million years ago, the first mammals appear.

Reader 19: 150 million years ago, very large birds emerge, direct descendants of the dinosaur.

Reader 20: 114 million years ago, flowers evolve, and insects fertilise plants on which they feed.

Reader 21: 65 million years ago, 5th mass extinction. Dinosaurs disappear and the age of mammals begins. Gradually, rodents, whales, monkeys, cats, dogs, horses, camels, elephants, chimpanzees, baboons and the first humans begin to appear.

Reader 22: 4 million years ago, hominids, (great apes) stand up and walk on two legs, these early creatures evolve into humans.

Reader 23: 100 thousand years ago, modern humans emerge.

Reader 24: 65 thousand years ago, ancestors of Australia's First Peoples begin to emerge in Australia.

Reader 25: 11,000 years ago, agriculture is invented. Humans begin to work with the environment.

Reader 26: 3,000 years ago, Religions emerge. Hinduism, Confucianism, Judaism, Buddhism, Christianity, Islam.

Reader 27: Around 250 years ago, scientists begin to calculate the Age of the Earth.

Reader 28: Around 85 years ago, for the first-time humans are aware they live in a developing universe.

Reader 29: Around 60 years ago, humans discover DNA, life's common language.

Reader 30: Around 50 years ago, Earth is seen as whole from space. Earth becomes complex enough to witness her own integral beauty.

Leader: Today, The Story of the Universe is being told as our sacred Story. The Flaring Forth continues as this moment. Pope Francis reminds us that Divine Love continues the work of Creation. (LS:80)
We are in awe and wonder with our sacred story.
All: We are in awe and wonder with our sacred story.
One by one, the candles are extinguished, and the space is cleared. Participants return inside sharing their experience of the ritual.

Reference: 'The Cosmic Walk' http://monmouthpresbytery.com/wp-content/uploads/pre2016-files/Genesis-Farm-Cosmic-Walk.pdf

Further Possibilities
*A large candle and 29 tea lights or small candles are required for this ritual. They are lit after each statement.
*In preparation, participants view 'How the Universe was Formed https://www.youtube.com/watch?v=s43lkwCsPPg

Awakening to Mysteries of the Universe

Deep Time Walk: a Walking History of Earth

Suitable for camps, reflection days, walking along the beach or other suitable times and places.

Note: Prior to participation, participants will download the award-winning app, 'Deep Time Walk – A New Story of Earth', which has been made available without charge on a gift-economy basis. Participants will use their device with headphones.

All gather in silence creating a large circle.

Leader: We acknowledge the Traditional Custodians of the land on which we gather, the _____ People. (Add in the name of local Indigenous group.) We recognise their continuing connection to land and community. We pay respects to Elders past, present and emerging.

Let us pause for a moment in silence. Feel your feet on the ground.

Pope Francis urges us to care for Earth our common home. Today, we are going to step back in time, an opportunity to experience a history of Earth like never before. By listening to 'Deep Time Walk', we will learn about key evolutionary events that have shaped Earth's 4.6-billion-year journey as they occur and comprehend the destructive impact of humans on Earth's complex climate. Yes, we will come to appreciate Earth our common home in a new way.

As you walk through time, use the dramatised audio narrative of the Deep Time Walk App, the story of Earth's formation. The narrative between a philosopher and a scientist combines the latest evidence with poetry to provide a unique and educational perspective of deep time.

For the next hour (*or time suitable*), we will simply walk and listen to Deep Time Walk and then gather back in our circle. You may not complete the journey today; however, we will come back to it at another time.

You are recommended to store your smartphone in your pocket when directed by the narrator. If you have earbuds, you may also wish to enable 'Gaiaphonic' audio mode, enabling one ear to be present to the world around you.

Participants begin walking and after an hour return to the circle.

Leader: We gather in the circle in silence once again.
As you reflect on your experience, is there anything you would like to share with the group?
It might be a question, a comment, a point of wonder or something else.
We will not comment on each one's sharing, simply listen.

After a suitable time, invite participants to repeat the following:

Leader: Yes, we appreciate Earth, our common home, in a new way.
All: Yes, we appreciate Earth, our common home, in a new way.

Reference: Information is gleaned from Deep Time Walk website: https://www.deeptimewalk.org/ and is used with permission. The Deep Time Walk App calculates your speed and distance as you journey across 4.6bn years of time, enabling you to learn about key evolutionary events as they occur and comprehend the destructive impact of humans on the Earth's complex climate. Students individually use the App.

Further Possibilities
*Prior to the Deep Time Walk experience, go to the website and familiarise yourself with the resources, complementing participants experience. These resources can also be used at other times.
    'Deep Time Line' A bookmark or memento of Earth's history for those participating in Deep Time Walk.
    'Deep Time Cards' 58 beautifully illustrated cards enable you to learn about Earth's history without any technology. They can be placed around the circle with participants reading aloud the 100 million year summary on each card.
    'The Script' A book of the narrative used in the App.

Awakening to Mysteries of the Universe

Star Gazing: Contemplating the Night Sky

A ritual suitable for school Camps and Retreats.

Gather outside when the sun is down, and the night sky is filled with stars.
Participants bring a mat, blanket or other suitable ground cover and lay on their back facing the night sky. Warm clothing will be necessary.

Leader: Make yourselves comfortable as you lie on your back gazing at the night sky.

Become aware of your breath and the evening temperature.

Yes, Pope Francis reminds us that the Spirit of God fills the universe. [LS:80]

Some of you may know Professor Brian Cox, often seen on television. He says, 'When we look out into space, we are looking into our own origins, because we are truly children of the stars.' How extraordinary!

Let's now begin our time of silent star gazing.

Notice the various colours, shapes and movements in the night sky. Let your imagination go wild. I will let you know when the time concludes.

At the conclusion, read the following.

Leader:
Yes, we are made of stardust.

When we look up at the stars, we see our own origins.

In our blood stream, we have hydrogen, created by the Great Flaring Forth.

We are indeed descendants of the Great Flaring Forth, 13.7 billion years ago.

Yes, we are all children of the stars. Amen.

All: Yes, we are all children of the stars. Amen.

Further Possibilities
*The experience may evoke, wonder, discussion and questions. Allow the conversations and questions to flow.
*Prior to this exploration, participants download the free App, 'SkyViewLite' - Exploring the Universe. When the App is open and tablet or phone is facing the night sky, names of stars, planets and constellations appear on the screen.
There may be other suitable free Apps available for download that identify star constellations and planets.
*Prior to this exploration, participants view 'Stargazing' ABC series with Brian Cox and Julia Zemiro. Google its availability.

We are Made of Star Dust, Connected to All that Is: We are Grateful

Leader: Today, we pause to remember that we are made of star dust, evolving from the primordial flaring forth 13.7 billion years ago. We, like all of creation, are deeply connected to everything that is. We have a role in the unfolding story of the universe.

Settle into a comfortable posture, with a straight back, feeling yourself on the chair and your feet on the ground. Become aware of your breathing.

The central candle is lit.

Reader 1: For Infinite Love within the creative process of all that is and, yes, within each of us.
All: We are grateful.

Reader 2: For the generations of supernovas that exploded, resulting in stars, eventually leading to the supernova that resulted in the solar system.
All: We are grateful.

Reader 3: For Mother Earth, continually evolving and ever generous in nurturing and giving.
All: We are grateful.

Reader 4: For soil, because of whom we can enjoy food, flowers, plants, clean air, shade and revelations of Divine Mystery.
All: We are grateful.

Reader 5: For those who work the land with respect, using sustainable and chemical-free farming methods.
All: We are grateful.

Reader 6: For the scientists, theologians, thinkers, writers, speakers, activists and artists who assist us to realise all of creation is interconnected and indeed sacred.
All: We are grateful.

Reader 7: For Pope Francis, reminding us of our innate connection with all of creation and our responsibility to wake up and take action in caring for Earth our Home.
All: We are grateful.

Leader: We are made of star dust, evolving from the primordial flaring forth 13.7 billion years ago. We, like all of creation, are deeply connected to everything that is.
We have a role in the unfolding story of the Universe. Amen.

All: Yes, we have a role in the unfolding story of the Universe. Amen.

Further Possibilities
*Prior to the ritual, participants research a scientist, theologian, thinker, writer, speaker, activist or artist. Their name and contributions are shared during the ritual. e.g. Jane Goodall, David Attenborough, David Suzuki.

Awareness of our Senses

Awareness of our Senses

Gratitude for our Five Senses

This meditation is suitable for inside and outside. Classroom, Camp, Reflection or Retreat.

Leader: We gather in this place in silence as we become aware of our sense of sight, hearing, smell, touch and taste.
Sit comfortably with your eyes closed and your hands in your lap. Relax your face and shoulders. Take a long deep breath and release. Repeat three times.
Come back to the natural rhythm of breathing and notice where you feel the air entering and leaving your body. Become aware of your body and notice any feelings or sensations.

Pause

Leader: We are aware of God, present in all that is.

The candle is lit.

Leader: We will now continue in silence for a moment before being led in a silent reflection using each of our senses.

A short silence

Leader: Become aware of any sounds you can hear close by and those in the distance. People talking, birds, traffic, wind movement and more. Simply allow yourself to listen carefully.

Pause

Leader: Now as you breathe through your nose notice different smells around you. It might be grass, the sea air, something cooking, nearby flowers. If you don't notice any smells, that's fine; simply focus on your breathing.

Pause

Leader: Now move your tongue around your mouth and notice any tastes. If you can't taste anything, that's fine; you might imagine eating your favourite food or simply focus on your breathing.

Pause

Leader: Now gently feel the clothing you are wearing and notice the texture. Touch the chair or grass you are sitting on and notice how they feel. Press your fingertips together and notice the sensation.

Pause

Leader: Remain in silence and slowly open your eyes. Become aware of what you see around you. Colours, shapes, items, movement, and other people. Simply notice.

Pause

Now take a deep long breath and release. Repeat three times.

Leader: We are grateful for our senses.
All: We are grateful for our senses.

Awareness of our Senses

Gratitude for the Gift of Hearing

Leader: We light this candle acknowledging the presence of Divine Mystery in, with, and around us.

Close your eyes and simply relax. During this time, we will pay attention to our gift of hearing. As you pay attention to your breathing, notice any sounds as the air comes in and out of your body.

Pause

Jesus said, 'Blessed be your ears for they hear.' Matthew 13:16

Leader: We will be still for a few moments simply listening. Relax your body and become comfortable. As you are quiet, notice the various sounds around you. They may be in the distance or nearby. They may be familiar or unknown.

Reader 1: Blessed be your ears for they hear.
All: Yes, we hear.

Reader 2: We hear Pope Francis' urgent call for all people to care for earth, our common home.
All: Yes, we hear.

Reader 3: We hear many people making daily positive choices respecting earth, our common home.
All: Yes, we hear.

Reader 4: We hear teen climate activists waking up young people and adults about our climate emergency.
All: Yes, we hear.

Reader 5: We hear our personal call to reflect on our daily choices and actions in our care for earth, our common home.
All: Yes, we hear.

Leader: Blessed be our ears for they hear the cry of the earth.
All: Blessed be our ears.

Further Possibilities
*Gather a variety of sounds, for example: a bell, the roaring sea, howling wind, sticks to bang together, a triangle, a phone ring, a baby crying, bird calls, animal noises and more. A selection could be played during the ritual as participants simply listen and notice.
*Choose a piece of music. Invite participants to get into a comfortable position as they relax and listen.
*Introduce a range of climate activists, including teens such as Greta Thunberg. Talk about the work they are doing and their inspiration for all young people. Invite participants to share what they have heard.

Awareness of our Senses

Gratitude for the Gift of Sight

Leader: We light this candle, acknowledging the presence of Divine Mystery in, with, and around us.

Leader: Today, we place our attention on the gift of sight.

Sit for a few moments in silence with your eyes open. Notice who is beside you and what is around you in this space.

Notice the candle in the centre and the flickering flame.

Let us say together. Blessed be the gift of sight.

All: Blessed be the gift of sight.

Reader 1: We see destruction where humanity has not respected Mother Earth.
All: We see destruction.

Reader 2: We see despair on the faces of those whose land is being lost due to climate emergency.
All: We see despair.

Reader 3: We see desperation where animals are under threat of extinction.
All: We see desperation.

Leader: We choose to open our eyes, noticing hope, encouragement and promise.

Reader 4: We see hope in the activities and decisions of those who care for Mother Earth.
All: We see hope.

Reader 5: We see encouragement from Pope Francis as he urges all to care for our common home.
All: We see encouragement.

Reader 6: We see promise in each one here committed to caring for Mother Earth.
All: We see promise.

Pause`

Leader: I invite you to turn to those beside you and look them in eye, and say:
Blessed are your eyes.
The person responds with: Blessed are my eyes.

Leader: Yes, blessed are our eyes. Amen.
All: Blessed are our eyes. Amen.

Further Possibilities
*Gather various pictures: the sea, night sky, stars, sunset, trees, mountains, animals, birds, fish, rivers, paddocks, snow, etc. These can be place in the centre of the circle around the candle or scattered amongst the participants.
*During the ritual, invite participants to focus on a picture. Invite a few to describe what they have seen followed by, 'How good to see the beauty of creation'.

Awareness of our Senses

Gratitude for the Gift of Smell

Leader: We light this candle, acknowledging the presence of Divine Mystery in, with, and around us.

The candle is lit.

We sit for a moment in silence as we prepare to become conscious of the gift of smell and express gratitude.

Leader: Today, we place our attention on the gift of smell. We experience a variety of smells through our day. Smells can bring back memories, alert us to danger and tantalise our taste buds.

Leader: Sit for a few moments in silence and concentrate on breathing through your nose. In and out. In and out. In and out. As you do this, notice the moment breathing in becomes breathing out and breathing out becomes breathing in.

Leader: We use our nostrils to breathe and to smell.

Imagine smelling your favourite hot drink.

Imagine smelling freshly baked bread.

Imagine smelling smoke from a woodfire.

Imagine smelling food cooking on a barbeque.

Imagine smelling crushed gum leaves.

Leader: We are in awe and wonder at our capacity to smell.
We are grateful for the gift of smell. Amen.

All: We are grateful for the gift of smell. Amen.

Further Possibilities
*Gather a variety of items, for example, bread, gum leaves, lavender, soap, fresh herbs, etc. Place them on small dishes in the centre of the circle or near the lit candle. They can be passed around during the ritual. Participants simply notice the difference in smells without words.
*Participants may be invited to name their favourite smell and ask others to imagine they can smell it now.

Awareness of our Senses

Gratitude for the Gift of Taste

Leader: We light this candle, acknowledging the presence of Divine Mystery in, with, and around us. We sit for a moment in silence as we prepare to delight in the gift of taste and express gratitude.

Pause

Reader 1: Jesus lived in harmony with creation and he enjoyed eating and drinking with his friends. A long time ago, Jesus shared bread and wine with his friends during their last meal together. He took the bread and wine and blessed it, and then shared it with his friends. Jesus said that every time you do this remember me.

All over the world, people share a variety of food and drink during meals, for various occasions.

Leader: As you sit in silence, with your eyes closed, bring to mind your favourite food. Imagine eating it and notice who is with you.

Leader: As you imagine yourself eating your favourite food, silently give thanks for the gift of taste.

Invite a few participants to share their experiences.

Reader 2: We give thanks for our taste buds found on our tongue that allow us to experience tastes that are sweet, salty, sour and bitter.

Leader: We are in awe and wonder at our capacity to taste. We are grateful for the gift of taste. Amen.

All: We are grateful for the gift of taste. Amen.

Further Possibilities
*Bring a variety of food and drink and have them ready to pass around during the ritual. As each one is passed around invite participants to taste it and share what they know about how each one is grown or made.

Awareness of our Senses

Gratitude for the Gift of Touch

Leader: We light this candle, acknowledging the presence of Divine Mystery in, with, and around us. We are grateful and delight in the gift of touch.

The candle is lit.

Leader: As you sit in silence for a moment, bring your hands together with fingertips touching. Notice your little fingers, your ring fingers, your middle fingers, your pointers and your thumbs. Gently press them together and become aware of the fine movement and gentle touching.

Pause

Open your palms and notice your fingertips and fingerprints.

Pause

Reader 1: Each of us is a unique spark of the universe. No two fingerprints are the same.
All: We are grateful and delight in the gift touch.

Reader 2: Our skin's ability to perceive touch sensations gives our brains a wealth of information about the environment around us, such as temperature, pain and pressure.
All: We are grateful and delight in the gift of touch.

Reader 3: Our skin, the largest organ in our body, contains five different types of touch receptors.
All: We are grateful and delight in the gift touch.

Pass around the various items from nature; in silence, participants take their time feeling the shape and texture of each one.

Leader: Let us now stand around the circle. [Name a participant] will begin and touch fingertips with the person on their left and that person with the person on their left until we are all connected by our fingertips.

We are grateful and delight in the gift of touch. Amen.

All: We are grateful and delight in the gift of touch. Amen.

Further Possibilities
*Gather a variety of items from nature and place them in the sacred space, for example stones, feathers, flowers, bark, fruits, vegetables, sand, leaves, sticks; and pass them around during the ritual inviting participants to take their time to feel the texture and shape of each one. Participants could be asked to close their eyes and identify the items by touch only.
*Participants research how our sense of touch works and share insights during the ritual.
*A small bowl of fragrant oil placed in the sacred space can be used for participants to bless each other's hands.

Awareness of our Senses

Mindfully Walking: Awakening the Senses

This reflection can be experienced on camp, on retreat, along the beach, the bush, on the school oval or other suitable location and time.

Leader: For the next 10 minutes (or time best suited to the age group), we will mindfully walk around in silence.

Reader: We acknowledge the Traditional Custodians of the land on which we gather, the _____ People. (Add in the name of local Indigenous group.) We recognise their continuing connection to land and community. We pay respects to Elders past, present and emerging.

Leader: As you walk slowly and attentively, notice each time you place your feet on the ground and remember the ground on which you stand is holy.

Tune into your sense of sight. As you walk, look around and notice the colours, shapes, textures, movements, sizes and contrasts of the many aspects of nature.

Now and then, stop and focus on one or two things and look a little closer.
Notice the different shades of the same colour, any movement from tiny insects, the various textures present, and other unexpected details.

Take your time. There is no rushing.

At the conclusion of the time you will hear a sound that will invite you back to the main group.

Begin your silent walk of noticing.

Silent Walking

Gather the group back in a circle.

Allow for stillness.

Pause

Leader: What are some of the things you noticed as you looked a little closer?

Invite spontaneous responses without discussion.

Leader: We walk with open eyes, noticing and appreciating nature in all her diversity.
Creative Presence is in, with and around us in all of creation. Amen.

All: Amen.

Further Possibilities:
*You can repeat this reflection with a focus on each of the senses.

Awareness of our Senses

Noticing Nature

This walking meditation is suitable for camps, reflection days, seasonal awareness, and other suitable times.

Gather participants outside in a circle.

Leader: As you stand in the circle, become aware of your feet on the ground.

Feel the air on your face.

Become still.

Notice any noises around you.

We are standing on holy ground and we acknowledge the Original Custodians of the land on which we gather, the _____ People.

Leader: In Laudato Si', Pope Francis tells us that nature is a constant source of wonder and awe. He says that nature continually reveals Divine Love to each of us.

Today, we will take some quiet time, wandering around in silence, simply noticing the natural world around us. The only thing you need to do is to notice what is around you.
After 10 minutes (*or a time best suited to the group*), I will ring the chime (*or other suitable gentle sound*) and we will gather back in the circle.

Gather participants back to the circle.

Leader: We stand in this circle in silence, appreciating Divine Love is present in the natural world around us.

Lead the participants to share what they noticed with the following structure.

| **Speaker 1:** | Today, I noticed the leaves on the ground. |
| **All:** | Divine Love is present in leaves. |

| **Speaker 2:** | Today, I noticed the sound of birds. |
| **All:** | Divine Love is present in birds. |

| **Speaker 3:** | Today, I noticed … |
| **All:** | Divine Love is present in … |

After several speakers, come to a natural conclusion and remain in silence.

Leader: Yes, Divine Love is present in the natural world.
All: Yes, Divine Love is present.

Further Possibilities
*An older class could invite a young class to join them for the walking, noticing meditation. Older students partner a younger student and together they walk and notice.
*Participants could take photos and create a book of images using the phrase 'Yes, Divine Love is present' under each image. These books could be shared with other groups and used as a reference for class prayer.
*Gather information on vegetation indigenous to your area. The ritual could be adapted, using and naming these plants.

Beginnings, Endings and Times In-between

Beginning the Day

This ritual is suitable for the classroom, assemblies, camp, reflection and retreat days, and other occasions.

Leader: Let us greet this new day together in silence.
In your silence, notice your in and out breath.
Notice when the in breath becomes the out breath and when the out breath becomes the in breath.

Silence

Leader: We are in awe of this day and grateful for the miracle of life.
We are in awe.
All: We are in awe.

Pause

Leader: We are encouraged and guided by many people who are inspired by Jesus' message of Love, Justice, Forgiveness and Inclusion.
We are encouraged.
All: We are encouraged.

Pause

Leader: We remember, Spirit of Love is in, with, and around us in everything that we do today.
We remember.
All: We remember.

Pause

Leader: We give thanks for this new day.
All: We give thanks for this new day.

Celebrating the Conclusion of Primary School

This ritual can be incorporated into an end of year reflection day or other suitable moment.

Leader:
We gather today, recognising that very soon each of you will be moving forward to year 7. You will be leaving this group and moving into another. Many of you will move together to the same school, some may move alone to another school. This time marks one of the many transitions you will make throughout your life.

Let's take some time to remember, celebrate and look forward.

Leader: As we light this candle, we acknowledge the presence of Divine Mystery in, with, and around us and all of creation.

Make yourselves comfortable and remain in silence. I will be asking you some questions and inviting you to share some of your responses. Sharing is voluntary. We won't be talking with each, however, simply listening and appreciating each one's uniqueness.

The time has come for each of you to leave primary school and move forward to secondary school. There are many things that you are proud of during your primary years. Take some time to think of one:
- perhaps you didn't give up on something you wanted to achieve;
- maybe you stood up for a friend;
- you surprised yourself with something you did; or
- you volunteered for something and learnt new things.

Take your time as you look back and remember.

Pause

Leader: Now return your attention to the group and focus on the candle. If you wish, share your memory with the group. Simply say, 'I remember, and I am proud of ...'
After each one speaks, we will remain silent. (*Each person can place a glass bead around the candle after they share.*)

When there is a natural conclusion, the leader continues.

Look around at each other, knowing that new adventures are ahead of you all.

Raise your right hand in blessing and repeat after me:
We acknowledge the presence of Divine Mystery in, with, and around us.
We give thanks for all that has been and open our hearts to all that is ahead of us. Amen.

Further Possibilities
*Have a collection of glass beads in a bowl by the lit candle. As the participant shares, they can place a glass bead around the candle. At the conclusion of the ritual each participant takes a bead, not necessarily the one they put down.
*This ritual can be adapted with the inclusion of further reflective questions. For example: What is the funniest memory of your time at primary school? Do you have a message for new students coming to primary school? What might be a challenge when you move to your new school? What excites you about moving into Year 7? Add further questions.

Beginnings, Endings and Times In-between

Circle of Hope: Setting Intentions

This ritual can be adapted and enacted for many occasions. For example, hopes for beginning the day, the week, term or year, World Environment Day, Intentions for our world, as a transition from primary to secondary school, transition from secondary to the next phase or any other occasion. The example below will focus on the beginning of the school year.

The group gathers in a circle. Two large sheets of paper surround a lit candle with the headings: 'My hopes for this Year' and 'Hopes for our Class.' There are sticky notes and pens/pencils nearby. The reading (John10:10) is also near the candle.

Leader: We gather in our circle of hope as we prepare for this new year together. You will notice the candle surrounded by two large sheets of paper. On one is written, 'My hopes for this Year'. On the other is written, 'Hopes for our Class.' During the ritual, you will listen and respond silently using the sticky notes and pens.

Make yourselves comfortable focusing on the central candle. Let us begin with a moment's silence. Notice your breathing. Become aware when the in breath becomes the out breath and when the out breath becomes the in breath.

Reader: *Step forward into the circle and pick up the reading.*
Jesus said, 'I have come that you may have life and have life to the full.' John 10:10
Pause, then slowly place the reading back by the candle.

Leader: We gather in this circle for the first time as we begin the year together. Yes, we want to live life to the full. Many of you know each other, some of you are new to the school. All of you are getting to know each other in a new way. You may have personal hopes and dreams for this year. You may also have hopes for the whole group. Take a moment to think about one thing you hope for yourself this year and write it on a sticky note. Adding your name on the note is optional.
Pause until all have completed.

Leader: I invite a few of you to name your hope and come forward and place it on the sheet. (*After about 5 have spoken invite others to come forward in silence and place their note on the sheet.*)

Leader: Now take a moment to think about a hope you have for the class as a whole and write it on a sticky note. Adding your name on the note is optional.
Pause until all have completed.

Leader: I invite a few of you to name your hope for the class and come forward and place it on the sheet. (*After about 5 have spoken, invite others to come forward in silence and place their note on the sheet.*)

Leader: We are grateful and blessed as we embark on our new year together. These hopes will be kept in our classroom and we will check in from time to see how we are going in manifesting our hopes and dreams. Yes, Jesus wants us to have life and have life in abundance, Amen.
All: Yes, life in abundance. Amen.

The candle is extinguished, and the notes are gathered and displayed in the classroom.
Alternately the notes could be typed up in large print for display.

Further Possibilities
*Students could also write their personal hopes in their journal and from time to time, they can check in on how they are going.

Create a Circle of Hope: Reflecting on Our Intentions

This reflection is to be used in conjunction with the previous ritual,
'Circle of Hope: Setting Intentions.'
This ritual can be used at the end of each week, midterm, end of term or year, as a way of reflecting on the intentions set during 'Circle of Hope: Setting Intentions' ritual.

The group gathers in a circle. The two large sheets of paper naming, 'My hopes for this Year' and 'Hopes for our Class' are placed in the centre beside the candle.

Leader: We gather in our circle of hope, remembering the hopes we set for ourselves and the hopes we set for our class. This is a time for us to check and see how we are going. During the ritual, you will listen and respond silently to the reflective questions.

Make yourself comfortable and focus on the central candle. Become aware of your breathing and allow yourself to relax.

Candle is lit.

We light this candle reminding us that we give human expression to Breath of Life.

Leader: Take a moment to recall the hopes you set for yourself earlier in the week/term/year. How are you going? How have your choices and actions contributed to achieving your hopes?
Pause

Leader: What are some things that you will continue to do and other things that you will do differently, contributing to bringing these hopes to reality?
Pause

Leader: How have your choices and actions contributed to the hopes set for the class earlier in the year?
Pause

Leader: What are some things that you will continue to do and other things that you will do differently, contributing to bringing these hopes to reality?
Pause

Leader: We acknowledge Creative Presence, in, with, and around us, as we work to bring our hopes to reality. Amen.

All: We acknowledge Creative Presence, in, with, and around us, as we work to bring our hopes to reality. Amen.

Further Possibilities
*As an alternative to silent reflection, invite the participants to write their responses in their journal. They can then refer to these from time to time and continue to check in with themselves and make new resolves.

Concluding Secondary Schooling: Reflection and Blessing

Leader: We gather today, recognising that your years of schooling have come to closure. Very soon each of you will be moving forward towards a new phase in your lives. Many adventures, challenges, surprises and possibilities are ahead of each of you.

Take a moment to settle into this space. Notice the natural rhythm of your breathing. In and out.

Reader 1: As we light this candle, we are silent. We reverence Divine Presence.

Leader: Make yourselves comfortable. I will be asking you some questions for your silent reflection. There is no need to share; simply remain with your thoughts.

Imagine your first day at school.
What is the name of the school? Who was with you and how were you feeling? Did you wear a uniform?
Imagine when you concluded primary school.
Who is a teacher you remember and why? What is something you did and thought you could never do?
Imagine when you began secondary school. Who were the important people around you and why?
Imagine yourself halfway through secondary school. What were you concerned about? What were you excited about? What surprised you about yourself?
Remain in your silence.
Now your schooling is concluding. Take a few moments to look back. There will have been times of challenge, confusion, excitement, wonder and achievement and much more. In your mind simply take your time to look back and remember.

Think about some of those people you wish to thank. It might be friends, teachers, parents, and other people who have believed in you and supported you during these years. In your mind, send them a blessing of gratitude.

Leader: Now return your attention to the group and the candle in the centre.

Reader 2: Jesus said, 'I have come that you may have life and have life in abundance' (John 10:10).

Leader: Raise your right hand in blessing and repeat after me:
> We acknowledge the presence of Divine Mystery in, with, and around us.
> We give thanks for all that has been and open our hearts to all that is ahead.
> We appreciate our interconnectedness with all that is.
> We commit to caring for Mother Earth as we live and grow.

Leader: Yes, may each of you have life, and life in abundance. Amen.
All: Yes, may each of us have life, and life in abundance. Amen.

Further Possibilities
*A small candle with the School logo could be given to participants during the ritual.
*This ritual can be extended with the inclusion of further reflective questions suitable to the group.
*This ritual could also be adapted and included into a school liturgy.
*Parents could be invited to this ritual with students in the centre circle and parents in the outer circle. You might include questions for parents related to their child's schooling.
*The questions could be prepared, and students are given some time to record reflections in their journals.

Beginnings, Endings and Times In-between

Daily Gratitude

This ritual can be celebrated at any time. Conclusion of the day, prior to bed at school camp, at the conclusion of a lesson, prior to a gathering, and other occasions.

Leader: We pause for moment to reflect on those things we are grateful for today.

Make yourself comfortable and relax your body.
Notice your breathing.
Notice the beginning, middle and end of your in breath.
Simply follow the natural rhythm of your breath.

The candle is lit.

Reader: We are human expressions of the greatest mystery of all, Divine Love.

Pause

Leader: Think back over your day. Focus your mind on something you are grateful for today.
It maybe time you spent with your friends, the lunch you enjoyed, a new experience, knowing there are people around you who care, the availability of fresh water, a kind word expressed to you and more. There is no right or wrong. This is your experience.

Pause

Leader: Let the many gifts you enjoyed flow through your mind and silently express gratitude.

Pause

Leader: Creator Spirit, we are grateful for our evolving universe and the gifts of each moment.
We are grateful.

All: We are grateful.

Further Possibilities
*Participants could be invited to write their reflections in their journal.

Beginnings, Endings and Times In-between

End of Year Reflection

This reflection is suitable for individual classes rather than in a large group. Taking time to pause and reflect over the year can provide an opportunity for students to: continue developing their reflective skills, acknowledge and celebrate accomplishments, bring understanding to challenges, and name those things they grateful for. Questions here can be adapted to meet the needs of the group.

Leader: Let us begin our time together in silence. Notice your breathing as you settle.

We light this candle, acknowledging Breath of Life within each of us.

Leader: As the year ends, we take some time in silence, to look back and appreciate all that has been. I'll ask you some questions and give you time to think about your responses. There is no need to share; you will simply recall your experiences in your mind. Make yourselves comfortable.

Leader: During this year, each of you has had a range of experiences, including challenges and highlights. Take a minute to recall some of your highlights. Think about what happened and why you remember these highlights.
Pause

Leader: There may have been some things that did not go so well for you this year. This is a normal part of life and learning. Take a minute to recall one of these moments and how you continued to move forward.

Pause

Leader: Many people, including adults and other students, have supported you in various ways during the year. Recall one or two people and in your mind thank them and tell them why you appreciate their support.

Pause

Leader: There will be many memories or moments that have been part of your year. There may be moments of laughter, moments of sadness, a time when you surprised yourself, a time when you stepped out of your comfort zone, a time when you spoke up for a friend, and much more. Allow some of these moments to come into your mind and express your gratitude.

Pause

Leader: As we conclude our reflection, we acknowledge Breath of Life, in, with and around us.
We give thanks.

All: We give thanks.

Further Possibilities
*The reflective questions could be incorporated into a memory book for the students where they record their experiences plus other highlights they wish to add. Alternatively, students record responses and reflections in their journal.
*Prior to asking the reflective questions, you may wish to give the students the option to share their responses in the larger group. After each sharing, there is no discussion.
*Students are given glass beads. Each time a question is asked, they hold one of the beads then place it in front of them when they have responded. The beads are then taken home.

Ending the Day

This ritual is suitable for the classroom, camp, reflection and retreat days, and other occasions.

Leader: As the day concludes, let us sit in silence for a few moments with eyes open or closed.

Leader: As you reflect on your day:

Think of something you are grateful for that happened today.

Pause

Is there something that surprised you today?
What was it and why did it surprise you?

Pause

What are you proud of today?
Perhaps a decision you made, an achievement, you had courage to speak up, or some other moment.

Pause

Is there something you will do differently tomorrow?

Pause

Leader: We give thanks for this day. We are grateful for the Spirit of Love, in, with, and around us.
We give thanks.

All: We give thanks.

Beginnings, Endings and Times In-between

Greeting a New Day

This ritual is suitable for the classroom, camp, reflection and retreat days and other occasions.

Leader: Let us greet this new day in silence.
In your silence, notice your breathing.
Notice when the in breath becomes the out breath and when the out breath becomes the in breath.

Silence

Leader: We give thanks for the gift of this new day.
All: We give thanks.

Leader: We give thanks for the many unknown opportunities that await us today.
All: We give thanks.

Leader: We give thanks for the many people who love us, inspire us, and want the best for us.
All: We give thanks.

Pause

Leader: We open our hearts and minds to Creative Energy of Love,
in, with and around us in everything that we do.
We open our hearts and minds today.
All: We open our hearts and minds today.

Gratitude and Blessing for our Food

Pausing before we eat.

We are thankful for sunshine enabling plants to grow.
We are thankful for rain and soil nurturing all growth.
We are thankful for those who attend to sustainable farming practices.
We are mindful that many people will go hungry today.
We give thanks and bless the food we are about to eat. Amen.

Beginnings, Endings and Times In-between

Greeting the Darkness: as Day Turns to Night

Suitable for camps when participants gather in thanks for the day.

All gather outside in silence, just before the sun light disappears below the horizon.

Leader: As we stand facing the west, we acknowledge the Traditional Custodians of the land on which we gather, the _____ People. (*Add in the name of local Indigenous group.*) We recognise their continuing connection to land and community. We pay respects to Elders past, present and emerging.

Pause

Reader 1:
We are in awe of the movement of Mother Earth.
As we stand here in silence, Mother Earth is spinning around and rotating around Brother Sun.
We are in awe.
All: We are in awe.

Pause

Reader 2:
We are in awe at the closure of this day created by a Divine Dance between Mother Earth and Brother Sun.
All: We are in awe.

Stand in silence as the colours of Brother Sun begin to move towards the horizon and eventually leave a glow.

Reader 3:
Raise your hands to the west towards Brother Sun and repeat after me:
We give thanks for the passing of light and evening rest.
All: We give thanks for the passing of light and evening rest.

Further Possibilities
*Check local time for 'sunset' and arrange for participants to gather 5-10 minutes beforehand.
*We often use the word 'sunset', the illusion of the sun setting beyond the horizon; however, we know that it is the rotation of earth around the sun that creates day and night.

Greeting the Light: as Night Turns to Day

Suitable for camps when participants rise early, greeting Brother Sun, as night turns to day.

All gather outside in silence, just before dawn, facing east.

Leader: Good morning to you all. Yes, an early gathering as we greet Brother Sun, on this new day.

Reader 1: As we stand facing the east, we acknowledge the Traditional Custodians of the land on which we gather, the _____ People. (*Add in the name of local Indigenous group.*) We recognise their continuing connection to land and community. We pay respects to Elders past, present and emerging.

Pause

Reader 2:
We are in awe of the movement of Mother Earth.
As we stand here in silence, Mother Earth is spinning around and rotating around Brother Sun.
We are in awe.
All: We are in awe.

Pause

Reader 3:
We are in awe of this new day created by a Divine Dance between Mother Earth and Brother Sun.
All: We are in awe.

Stand in silence as the Brother Sun begins to colour the sky with light.

Reader 4:
Raise your hands towards Brother Sun and repeat after me:
We give things for the light of this new day.
All: We give thanks for the light of this new day.

Further Possibilities
*Check local time for 'sunrise' and arrange for participants to gather 5-10 minutes beforehand.
*We often use the word 'sunrise', the illusion of the sun rising above the horizon; however, we know that it is the rotation of earth around the sun that creates day and night.

Pause, Reflect and Give Thanks for the Day

This ritual can be celebrated at the end of a school day, at camp or reflection day.

Gather the students and together take some time to recall the events of the day.

Bring the group to silence.

Leader:
As we gather in silence at the end of this day, notice your breathing. In and out. In and out.

Now close your eyes and we will sit silently for… minutes as we take time to recall the events of the day with some guided questions.

As I read the question, simply reflect silently on what comes to your mind.

Leader:
What have you enjoyed most during this day at school/camp/retreat and why?

Pause

What has surprised you about yourself today?

Pause

Is there something that you have done for the first time today? What was it and how did you go?

Pause

In your mind, express gratitude for the experiences of this day.

Pause

Leader:
Jesus said, 'I have come that you may have life and have life in abundance' John 10:10
We give thanks for the abundance of this day.

All: We give thanks for the abundance of this day.

Further Possibilities
*The reflective questions, or others suited to the group, could be prepared on a handout sheet with pens available. Students could record their responses and be invited to share aloud at the end of each moment of silent reflection. Be sure to emphasise that sharing is not compulsory.
*Participants could be given time to record their reflection in their journals.

Beginnings, Endings and Times In-between

Remembering the Day

Based on the daily Examen of St Ignatius.

Leader: Take a moment to become still.
You might choose to close your eyes.
Feel your body on the chair or floor.
Notice your breathing.

Reader 1: As we gather today, we remember we are human expressions of Breath of Life.

The candle is lit.

Leader: As a way of remembering our day I will ask you some questions. You do not need to share; simply think about your responses in your mind.

Leader: What are you most thankful for today?
Think of your day and recall one moment that you are happy about.
Who was there, what was said or done to make it good?
Take a moment to be grateful.

Leader: Remember a moment when you made a positive difference to others.
Did you smile at another person?
Were you generous when asked to share ideas?
Did you respond to others with kindness?

Leader: Was there a moment when you could have done something differently?
Who was there, what was said and what happened?
Remember the moment without trying to fix it.
Let go of this moment now and know new things are possible.

Leader: Give thanks for your day and your experiences.
Today I am grateful for... because...

Leader: Looking forward to tomorrow.
Think about tomorrow.
There will be many unknown choices and experiences ahead of you.
Open your mind and heart to the gift of tomorrow.

Leader: We are human expressions of Breath of Life, in our kindness, forgiveness and welcoming of each other. We are grateful for this day.
All: We are grateful for this day.

Further Possibilities
*Participants are given a copy of the reflection questions and in silence record their responses in their journals.

Beginnings, Endings and Times In-between

Welcoming Students to Primary School

This ritual is suited for incorporation into the first school liturgy or assembly for the year.

Leader 1: As we light this candle, we are silent. We reverence Divine Presence within all of us gathered here today.

We are excited because we have a number of new students joining our school community.

Pause

Leader 2: Scripture shares many stories of Jesus greeting and welcoming people. He met them with an open, loving heart. Jesus acknowledged that we all belong to one big human family. Yes, that means all of us. We belong to one big human family. One of the groups in our human family is _____ school/college.

Leader 1 : I invite all those new to _____ school/college to stand.

Leader 2: We welcome you. Each of you now forms a unique part of _____ school/college community.

Leader 1: I invite others gathered to raise their right hand in blessing and repeat after me.

> We look forward to getting to know you.
> Bless you.
>
> We hope you have lot of fun and make new friends here.
> Bless you.
>
> May your individual spark of life and creatively flourish.
> Bless you.

Leader 2: I invite you all now to sit as we continue our liturgy.

Further Possibilities
*Incorporate within the ritual the gift of a small tube stock plant for each of the students. With each plant include the name, care instructions and an invitation to plant it at home where they can care for it and nurture its growth. Or alternately there may be an area within the school for planting. Perhaps assign an older student as a 'buddy' and together they care for the plant.

Welcoming Students to Secondary School

This ritual is suited for incorporation into the first school liturgy or assembly for the year.

Leader 1: As we light this candle, we are silent. We reverence Divine Presence within all of us gathered here in this place today.

We are excited because we begin a new year with many students joining our school community for the first time.

Leader 2: Scripture shares many stories of Jesus greeting and welcoming people. He met them with an open, loving, heart believing in the goodness of all people. Jesus acknowledged that we all belong to one big human family. Yes, that means all of us. One of the groups in our human family is _____ school/college.

Leader 1: I invite all those new to _____ school/college to stand.

Leader 2: We welcome you, as you each now form a unique part of _____ school/college community.

Leader 1: I invite others gathered to raise their right hand in blessing and repeat after me.

> We look forward to getting to know you.
> We bless you.
>
> We wish you love, laughter and belief in your own goodness.
> We bless you.
>
> May your individual spark of life and creativity flourish.
> We bless you.

Leader 2: I invite you all now to sit as we continue our liturgy.

Further Possibilities
*Gather the names of the schools students previously attended and acknowledge these within the ritual. From many communities a new one is created in this new setting.
*Incorporate within the ritual the gift of a small tube stock plant for each of the students. With each plant, include the name, care instructions and an invitation to plant it at home where they can care for it and nurture its growth or, alternately, there may be an area within the school for planting. Students care for these throughout their schooling.

Called to Action

Called to Action

Animals under Threat of Extinction: Creating a Mandala

Note: Prior to the ritual, either in threes, pairs or alone, participants choose a country and investigate creatures that are under threat of extinction. The images and names of the creatures are copied, together with information ready for the creation of a mandala. The creation of the mandalas is best suited to outside or in a large indoor space.

Leader: We gather today to bring to our attention that many animals, fish and birds around the world are under treat of extinction. Are there any that you know about?

Invite sharing and discussion prior to the lighting of the candle.

Reader: As we light the central candle, we share a message of Pope Francis in Laudato Si', On Care for our Common Home: Each creature reflects something of God. How then can people possibly mistreat them or through a desire for profit, destroy their habitat so that they become extinct. [LS:221]

Leader: You have been gathering information and images about animals, fish and birds around the world that are under threat of extinction. Let us go around the circle and share the name of your chosen creature and a sentence about why they under threat of extinction.

At the conclusion of the sharing:
Inquire from the group what they know about mandalas. Many will have seen or created mandalas in other settings. You can use information below or your own information plus a PowerPoint or printed images of various mandalas.

The word mandala comes from the Sanskrit meaning 'circle'. The mandala is one of humankind's most ancient art forms. Various types of mandalas may be found in several religions, cultural art forms and in architecture. In churches we often find stunning mandalas in the form of the rose window, a circular, stained-glass design symbolising many stories. A mandala is generally circular with symmetrical features, often telling a story in images or symbols or simply a creative expression of the moment.

Leader: You will now work in threes, pairs or alone and create a mandala of your chosen animal under threat of extinction. Use the images you have collected, related information, signs, symbols and other creative expressions. You will have plenty of time to complete your mandala. It is fine to talk softly as you create.

Conclusion:
By way of conclusion, invite the students to walk around in silence appreciating the various mandalas created by their colleagues.

Gather the group together. Allow for sharing of their experience.

Leader: We honour Creative Energy flowing uniquely through each of us today.
We lament that many creatures around the world are under threat of extinction.
Yes, we know that every creature reflects something of God. Amen.
All: Yes, we know that every creature reflects something of God. Amen.

Further Possibilities
*At the conclusion, participants can take a photo of their mandala and a book could be created: 'Lamenting: Creatures under threat of Extinction.' Or the images could be laminated and an 'Awareness Wall' created in an appropriate location in the school together with names and information.
*Google and gather several images of mandalas to create a PowerPoint. Use these images during the ritual together with a shared understanding of mandalas.

Celebrating What We Do to Make a Difference in the World

Leader: We gather today, to name the things we are concerned about in the world and to reflect on those things we can do to make a difference.
Let us begin with a minute of silence.
Notice your breathing. Notice the moment the in breath becomes the out breath.
Notice the moment the out breath becomes the in breath.

Reader 1: We gather on holy ground acknowledging Creative Energy, in, with and around us.

The candle is lit.

Reader 2: Plastic is killing turtles, birds, fish, platypus and other creatures.
All: We are concerned.

Reader 3: Rivers are being polluted by chemicals that destroy ecosystems.
All: We are concerned.

Reader 4: Trees are being cut down to make way for development.
All: We are concerned.

Reader 5: Many broken items are thrown 'away' and end up in landfill.
All: We are concerned.

Reader 6: Pope Francis has said we must believe that we can make a difference to change the world, and indeed we must. He suggests that even our smallest efforts do make a difference and can bring forward goodness in others to do the same. [LS:212)]

Pause

Reader 7: Refilling our water bottle reduces plastic waste.
All: We make a difference.

Reader 8: Caring for and respecting our own belongings builds responsibility.
All: We make a difference.

Reader 9: Refusing to buy clothing made in sweat shops slowly reduces demand.
All: We make a difference.

Reader 10: Only buying and using what we need reduces excess and waste.
All: We make a difference.

Leader: All the earth and everything within her is sacred. We make a difference when our actions are respectful, mindful and conscious of our shared responsibility. Yes, we make a difference.
All: Yes, we make a difference.

Called to Action

Changing the Way We View Mother Earth

Leader: Today, we focus on changing the way we view Mother Earth.
Yes, all the world is sacred and indeed very good.

Let us pause for a moment, becoming still and calm, focusing on our breathing. Notice the gentle in and out rhythm of your breath.

Reader 1: We light this candle to acknowledge the presence of Divine Energy permeating all that is.

The candle is lit.

Pause

Reader 2: Let us see mountains as majestic beings amongst us, not just as a mound of ore to be extracted.

Pause

Reader 3: Let us see rivers as veins flowing across the earth and a home for many, not only as possible water for farming and agriculture.

Pause

Reader 4: Let us see the bush and the forests as shelter and home to various creatures, not just as potential building materials nor logs for fires.

Pause

Reader 5: Let us see all creatures of earth as 'biological kin' and not as potential for our use, mistreatment or dominance.

Pause

Leader: Invite the students to create their own awareness line, 'Let us see…

Pause

Leader: Let us view the world with new eyes. Yes! All the world is indeed sacred in our eyes! Amen.
All: Yes! All the world is indeed sacred in our eyes. Amen.

This ritual is inspired by the writings of David Suzuki and a song by Peter Kearney.

Further Possibilities
*Begin and/or conclude the ritual listening to the song, 'All the World is Sacred' by Peter Kearney. Links are below.
 'All the World is Sacred' (Track 2) can be auditioned and downloaded at the following site: https://store.cdbaby.com/cd/peterkearney5 Peter Kearney Website with further works by Peter: http://www.peterkearneysongs.com.au/
*Students create their own collage of photos taken from the natural environment within the school. Encourage them to take close-up photos showing the intricacies of the plant, tree or grasses, changing the way they view nature within the school yard. These pictures can be mounted with the words, 'All the world is Sacred' as its heading.
*Prior to the ritual, participants can be given one of the phrases used and they collect images reflecting the phrase. These images are placed around the sacred space during the ritual.

Called to Action

Earth Hour - Switch off - Connect to Earth

Earth Hour is marked throughout the world on March 30th.
This ritual can be celebrated at any time at school, on camp or retreat.
This ritual is based on information from Earth Hour Website. www.earthhour.org.au

Leader: As we sit together with lights off and technology put away, we connect with others around the world showing our commitment to act and care for Mother Earth.

We pause in silence as we light the candle, reminding us of the original flaring forth from which everything that is has evolved.
We are mindful of Divine Love permeating all that is.

Reader 1: We know that every action we make impacts positively or negatively on the environment.

Reader 2: Australia is home to some of the world's most iconic and breathtaking natural landscapes and wildlife; however, the current climate emergency is putting all this at risk.

Reader 3: Pope Francis says, 'Let's tackle the climate emergency together to care for earth our common home'. He says every one of us can cooperate using our unique skills and talents for the care of creation. He says every positive action, no matter how small, can make a difference. cf.[LS:14]

Pause

Leader: 'Every year, hundreds of millions of people around the world in more than 7,000 cities in over 180 countries take part in this amazing global conservation movement, Earth Hour. People do a wide range of things around the hour to show they care about the planet's future. Millions choose to mark Earth Hour by going 'lights out' for 60 minutes at 8.30pm – a symbolic show of solidarity.' www.earthhour.org.au

Invite participants to stand.

Reader 4: We too stand up as sign of solidarity with people around the world. We are part of this amazing global conservation movement Earth Hour, and we commit to positive action towards care for earth our common home.

Leader: As we stand in silence, we send blessings to all people who are waking up and making a positive difference in their care for earth, our common home.
Blessed be those who wake up and make a difference. Amen.

All: Blessed be those who wake up and make a difference. Amen.

Further Possibilities
*Go to the Earth Hour website:www.earthhour.org.au, and check the focus for the year for incorporation into the ritual.
*The Earth Hour website has links for schools and community involvement. There are also many short informative video clips that could be used prior to or during the ritual.
*Cool Australia – Learn for Life Website. https://www.coolaustralia.org/ Downloadable units of work related to Earth Hour are available and are linked to Australian Curriculum Standards.
*At the conclusion of the ritual, participants plan an electricity- and technology-free hour.

Called to Action

Global School Climate Reflection

Greta Thunberg, Swedish climate activist, 'a schoolgirl climate change warrior', has acted on her beliefs. Through her single action of sitting with a sign outside Stockholm's Parliament House – 'School strike for Climate' – she has initiated a global movement wanting people to feel the fear she feels each day about our global catastrophe and then wants them to act. Greta says, 'Some people can let things go. I can't.'

Greta says that she was the girl in the back of class who didn't say anything. She thought she couldn't make a difference because she was too small. Now more than a year after her lone act as a 15 years old, with an active following by students worldwide, addressing international audiences, Greta is a model of determination, inspiration and positive action. 'You are never too small to make a difference,' says Greta Thunberg.

Leader: We gather today, grateful for the inspiration of Greta Thunberg and mindful of our own capacity to act and make a positive difference for our world. We begin in silence, getting comfortable and noticing our breathing. The candle is lit as we reverence Divine Presence.

Reader 1: We are aware that Jesus was moved by Love in seeking justice, equity, forgiveness and inclusion as he went about his daily life.
All: We are aware.

Reader 2: We are aware that the same Spirit of Love runs through each us in the ordinary and extraordinary moments of our day.
All: We are aware.

Reader 3: We are aware that the same Spirit of Love permeates every creature, every plant, every bird, every star and every rainbow.
All: We are aware.

Reader 4: We give thanks for Greta who has shown us that one small action can and does make a difference to our world.
All: We give thanks.

Reader 5: We are conscious of our capacity to be determined to make a difference.
All: We are conscious.

Reader 6: We are conscious of our capacity to inspire others to see things differently.
All: We are conscious.

Reader 7: We are conscious of our capacity to take positive action contributing to care for earth, our common home.
All: We are conscious.

Leader: We are grateful for the inspiration of Greta. We are committed to wake up and become conscious of our actions towards care for Mother Earth. Amen.
All: We are committed. Amen.

Further Possibilities
There are many YouTube clips available to show the group before the ritual as a way of warming them up to the theme. In your capacity as a teacher you may well elicit discussion with your students.
Greta's address to the United Nations Negotiators and climate activists at the summit in Poland 17th Dec. 2018 https://climatesafety.info/meet-2018s-climate-oracle/
Acknowledgment: Information on Greta Thunberg used in the introduction cited: https://www.theguardian.com/world/2019/mar/11/greta-thunberg-schoolgirl-climate-change-warrior-some-people-can-let-things-go-i-cant

Called to Action

My Choices Make a Difference: a Reflection

This reflection can be used at any time, including end of the day, retreat days and camps.

Leader: Today, we take a few moments to reflect on some of the choices we have made during the day.

Make sure you are in a comfortable position. Become aware of those around you and then take a few full deep breaths to settle into this moment. As you breathe, place your hand over your heart, acknowledging life-giving blood moving through your body. Gently place your hands in your lap.

Reader 1: We light this candle and remember that Jesus often went to a quiet place where he could be alone and pray. [Luke 5:16]

Leader: Like Jesus, we now take some time out to reflect on how we are living our lives.

Pause

Reader 2: Pope Francis reminds us that everything is interconnected including the decisions we make each day. [LS:138]

Reader 3: What we buy, what we eat, what we say, what we do, all make a difference to others and the natural world.

Pause

Leader: I will now ask you a few questions to reflect on. You do not need to share; simply think about your response in your mind or record your reflections in your journal.
Allow enough time between questions.

Leader: How did a choice you made today harm the environment or enhance the environment?

Leader: How did a choice you made today discourage and cause sadness to another or encourage and bring happiness to another person?

Leader: How did a choice you made today contribute to non-caring action or reflect your belief that all the earth is sacred?

Leader: How did a choice you made today cause others to be surprised by your courage?

Leader: We are grateful for this time of reflecting on choices we make. We acknowledge the presence of Infinite Love in, with, and around us always. Amen.
All: Amen.

Further Possibilities
*Participants could use their journals to respond to these reflective questions.

Called to Action

Reflecting on our Daily Choices.
Building up or Breaking down Mother Earth

A short-guided reflection.

Gather in a large circle.

Leader: Stand and pause in silence for a moment.

We stand on Holy Ground, knowing that all of earth is sacred.

Pause for a minute.

Leader: In a moment, I will ask you some questions for your reflection. You don't need to share your response with anyone. Simply be with your own inner thoughts.

Reader: *Take a step into the circle and say slowly:* Pope Francis urges us to make daily decisions that contribute positively towards evolving Mother Earth. [LS:79]

Pause

Reader: *Take another step into the circle and say it again slowly:* Pope Francis urges us to make daily decisions that contribute positively towards evolving mother earth. [LS:79]

Pause

Leader: Now, take a moment to think back over your day.

Leader: We are aware that everything we buy, eat, do and say has consequences for Mother Earth. We either build up or break down Mother Earth many times during the day.

Leader: Pause for a moment and think about some of the choices you have made today.

Pause for a few moments.

Leader: Did your choices do harm to Mother Earth or did they contribute positively to her?
Pause
Leader: What is something you could do differently tomorrow?
Pause

Leader: We stand on Holy Ground knowing that all of earth is sacred.

All: We stand on Holy Ground knowing that all of earth is sacred.

Further Possibilities
 *A globe of the world is placed in the sacred space surrounded by a variety of pictures of creatures, people, and the environment. Some images showing destruction; and others positive care for Mother Earth.
*Create a list of choices that are part of everyday life. Beside each choice the group brainstorm responses that contribute positively towards Mother Earth. A list is compiled and displayed in the classroom. At the end of each day, pause and ask, 'How did we go making positive choices towards Mother Earth today?'
*Participants could have a journal and record their responses to the reflection and their commitment to do something differently. Each day, they check in with themselves and record how they went with their choices and commitment to something differently.

Random Acts of Kindness Make a Difference

Leader:	Let us gather in silence for one minute. Become aware of the natural rhythm of your breath.
	Pause
Reader1:	Pope Francis reminds us that everything is related and that we are all woven together by God's Divine Love. [LS:92]
Leader:	As we light our central candle, we remember: yes, we are all woven together with Divine Love.
	Pause
Reader2:	Jesus said to those around him, 'Love one another just as I have loved you.' John 13:34-35
	Pause
Reader 3:	A small act of kindness, an act of love, can surprise someone and touch their mind and heart deeply.
	Pause
Reader 4:	A small act of kindness, an act of love, can make a positive difference to others and our world in ways we may never know.
	Pause
Reader 5:	A small act of kindness, an act of love, can show another person that love is possible when perhaps they doubted.
	Pause
Reader 5:	Pause for a moment and think about something that you can do for another person today as a small act of kindness.
	Pause
Leader:	Yes, we are all woven together with Divine Love.
All:	Yes, we are all woven together with Divine Love.

The World Can't Wait.
A Message from Pope Francis

Leader: Pope Francis has written a letter addressed to every person on Planet Earth.
The letter is titled, Laudato Si' – On Care for our Common Home. The focus of his letter is asking every one of us to wake up and protect Mother Earth, our common home.

Reader 1: As the candle is lit, we recall Pope Francis message that Divine Love is in, with, and around Mother Earth with beauty and wonder everywhere.

Reader 2: Pope Francis wants us to wake up and tells us:
Mother Earth and all within her belongs to everyone.
Sadly, today our common home has been hurt and mistreated.
Human development has expanded enormously.
Mother Earth has been treated as though her resources are unlimited.
Much of the earth's natural forests have been cut down.
A great deal of water has been polluted.
Many creatures are losing their natural habitats.
Mother Earth has large areas of garbage where once there was beauty.
Pause

Reader 3: Pope Francis' message is urgent.
We are using more and more fossil fuel which is contributing to the climate disaster.
Climate change affects us all but sadly it is often the poorest communities who suffer the most.
Even though we have these problems most people are not slowing down how much they buy and throw away. A trail of waste and destruction is present.
Pope Francis says we cannot continue to live like this.

Reader 4: Pope Francis knows we can change and make a new beginning in our care for Mother Earth.
He is calling for the whole human family to work together to care for our planet earth.
He is calling us to plant beauty not destruction.
He says, 'Let us put our love for the world and love for our neighbours into action by living together in harmony and caring for nature.'

Reader 5: We all know some simple everyday action to care for the earth like:

Reader 6: Turning off lights when they are not needed.

Reader 7: Being careful with our use of water.

Reader 8: Recycling paper, bottles, cans and other products.

Reader 9: Reducing the number of things we buy and throw away, not taking more than we really need.

Leader: Pope Francis says, 'The world can't wait.'
We commit to care for Earth, our Common Home. Amen.

All: We commit to care for Earth, our Common Home. Amen.

Adapted from 'Laudato Si' animation for Children. CAFOD https://cafod.org.uk/Education/Primary-teaching-resources/Laudato-Si-animation

The World is in Need of Healing. A Prayer of Lament

Leader: Jesus shared his dream for the world. A world of peace, justice, forgiveness, happiness, and where care for each other and for earth is present.
Let us pause in silence for one minute as we realise our world is in need of healing.

Pause

Right side: We lament that people die because of war and terrorism and that the physical and mental scars live on through generations.
All: We lament.

Right side: We lament that humankind continues to struggle to solve world issues through destructive means.
All: We lament.

Right side: We lament that we can hurt each other in the words we say and words we don't say in critical moments.
All: We lament.

Right Side: We lament that some of our friends and colleagues have few people around them who believe in them and encourage them.
All: We lament.

Reader: Jesus said, 'You shall love God, with all your heart, and with all your soul, and with all your mind, and with all your strength. You shall love your neighbour as yourself.'
cf. Matthew 22:37

Left Side: We remember that our world is created for all people, creatures and vegetation to live in harmony.
All: We remember.

Left Side: We remember that our friendships are based on the greatest commandment – to love one another as God loves us, to treat all people with respect and to honour the human person with dignity.
All: We remember.

Left Side: We remember that we have the capacity to be the peace we want to see in our school, with our families and the world through our everyday words, thoughts, and actions.
All: We remember.

Leader: As we go about our day, let us remember to be the peace we wish to see in our world.
Amen.
All: Amen.

© 'Sparks of the Universe' Jennifer Callanan

We Lament Australian Animals under Threat of Extinction

Leader: Make yourselves comfortable. Become still and focus your eyes on the candle in the centre of the circle.

Reader 1: We light this candle today, remembering that Divine Love is present in all of creation. We also remember that many animals in Australia and around the world are under threat of extinction.

Reader 2: Australia is home to some of the most extravagant, eccentric and dangerous animals. Sadly, Australia has the highest rate of animal extinction in the world. We know that all species are important to the eco-system and when we lose a species, we lose their ecological role; in other words, their unique role in creation. This is devastating.

Leader: Today, we will name and lament 5 of the 300 plus endangered animals at risk of extinction here in Australia. When we lament together, we express our common sadness.

Reader 3: We lament the Black-flanked Rock-wallaby, once widespread across many parts of Western Australia, South Australia and the Northern Territory, is now endangered.
All: We lament.

Reader 4: We lament the Eastern Curlew, spotted in north-eastern and southern Australia, is now endangered.
All: We lament.

Reader 5: We lament the Gouldian Finch, perhaps the most beautiful small bird in the world, is now endangered.
All: We lament.

Reader6: We lament the Northern Quall, occurring from the Pilbara region of Western Australia across the Northern Territory to south east Queensland, is now endangered.
All: We lament.

Reader 7: We lament the Black-footed Tree-rat, found in north-east Queensland and parts of the Northern Territory, is now endangered.
All: We lament.

Leader: We remember Divine Love is present all of creation.
All: We remember Divine Love is present in all of creation.

Reference: The Nature Conservancy Australia.
https://www.natureaustralia.org.au/explore/australian-animals/australia-s-endangered-animals/

Further Possibilities
*Prior to the ritual, participants could research one of the above creatures. They could bring an image and share information during the ritual.
*In small groups, students are assigned a country to research and focus on the extent of potential animal extinction in that country. They can then create a ritual of lament using the above as a model. The rituals can be shared over time within the class group or wider community. A collection of the rituals of lament could be bound together and gifted to each of the classes within the school.

Celebrating the Elements

Celebrating the Elements

In Thanks for Air

Leader: Close your eyes and breathe in and out through your nose and become aware of your breath. Take a deep breath, hold it for a few seconds and then release. Do this a few times.
Yes, we, and all of creation, depend on brother air for survival.

The candle is lit.

Leader: Breath of Life sustains us and all of creation.

Now relax your body, with your hands in a comfortable position and return to the natural rhythm of your breathing. Place your hands in front of your mouth and feel the air as you breathe in and out.

Reader 1: Air contains just the right balance of nitrogen, oxygen, argon, carbon dioxide and small amounts of other gases to sustain us and all of creation. The balance of nature is delicate.

Pause

Reader 2: When air is polluted, many crops are damaged. We lament.
All: We lament.

Reader 3: A large amount of the world's population live in places with unhealthy air quality. We lament.
All: We lament.

Reader 4: People develop diseases and are dying when living with polluted air. We lament.
All: We lament.

Pause for a moment.

Reader 5: We are mindful that many people are committed to clean up the air we breathe, by using environmentally friendly practices. We are grateful.
All: We are grateful.

Reader 6: We are mindful that as trees grow, they cleanse polluted air by removing the carbon dioxide, storing carbon in the trees and soil, and releasing oxygen into the atmosphere. We are grateful.
All: We are grateful.

Reader 7: We are mindful that those who care for earth, our home, are working towards plans to prevent further air pollution. We are grateful.
All: We are grateful.

Leader: Yes, we, and all of creation, depend on brother air for survival. We commit to care for earth, our common home. Amen.
All: We commit to care for earth, our common home. Amen.

Further possibilities
*Participants research major air pollutants and their effect on the environment. During the ritual, include a space where participants share their findings. A further ritual of lament could be created with their findings.

In Thanks for Fire

Gather inside around a candle or outside around a firepit or large candle.

Leader: At Pentecost, the symbol of fire is used to remind us of God's Divine Love for all people.

Today we light this fire/candle, knowing that God's Divine Love is present in, with and around us.
Let's sit in silence for a few moments.
Simply focus your eyes on the fire/candle.

Reader 1: We are aware that fire cannot exist without oxygen.

Reader 2: We are amazed that fire continues to burn in the centre of the earth.

Reader 3: We realise the destructive capacity of fire.

Reader 4: We know that earth is the only planet where fire can burn.

Reader 5: We learn from First Nations people who cared for country using fire in land management to regenerate flora.

Reader 6: We understand many people are now learning how the use of fire can be adopted for a variety of land management problems.

Reader 7: We appreciate the warmth of fire.

Leader: Let's sit in silence for a few moments. Simply focus your eyes on the fire/the flame of the candle.

Leader: We are grateful for fire.
All: We are grateful for fire.

Further Possibilities
Participants research the use of fire in indigenous cultures in regulating land management.

Celebrating the Elements

In Thanks for Soil

Leader: We gather in silence for a few moments. Notice your breathing. Gently in and out.

As we light this candle, we are silent. We reverence Divine Presence.

Pause

Side 1: Three quarters of our planet is covered with water including lakes, oceans, rivers and icecaps.

Side 2: We live on the quarter of the planet covered with earth, soil, dirt and ground, whatever we call it.

Side 1: Vegetables and fruits are dependent on the goodness of soil for healthy growth.

Side 2: Animals that give us food rely on the health of the soil to produce grains and grasses.

Side 1: Animals in the wild depend on the seasons for soil to nurture and grow some of their food.

Side 2: Flowers, with their roots in the soil, provide beauty for all and pollen for the bees.

Side 1: Trees have lived for hundreds of years with their roots going deeply into the soil for support and nourishment.

Side 2: Soil provides a home for many tiny creatures.

Leader: We are grateful for the gift of soil.
All: We are grateful for the gift of soil.

Further Possibilities
*Have a bowl of soil in the centre of the sacred space beside the candle.
*Prior to the ritual, gather images for each of the statements. These images are placed in the sacred space as the statement is read.
*Participants research the various creatures that live in the soil assisting in maintaining its health.
*Plant some herbs or flowers in pots. These are then cared for by the gathered group.

Celebrating the Elements

In Thanks for Water

This ritual can be used celebrating World Day of Water – March 22nd – or at any other time.

Leader: Find yourself a comfortable position. We begin with a moments silence as we prepare to celebrate the wonderful gift of water.

As we light this candle, we listen to the words of Pope Francis from Laudato Si', On Care for Our Common Home.

Reader 1: 'Fresh drinking water is an issue of primary importance, since it is indispensable for terrestrial and aquatic ecosystems.' [LS:28]

Reader 2: Water is the only substance naturally found on earth in three different forms: as liquid, vapour (gas) or ice (solid). We give thanks for gift of water.
All: We give thanks for the gift of water.

Reader 3: Water alters our landscape in more ways than we realise. We give thanks for the power of water.
All: We give thanks for the power of water.

Reader 4: Rivers and streams readily pick up nutrients and salts, transporting them great distances, much like our own circulatory system. We give thanks for rivers and streams.
All: We give thanks for rivers and streams.

Reader 5: Ocean currents regulate global climate by transporting warm water from the equator towards the poles, and cold water back to the tropics. We give thanks for ocean currents.
All: We give thanks for ocean currents.

Reader 6: Trees transpire far more water than they use to grow. Water is released as vapour through a plant's leaves. We give thanks for the cycle of transpiration.
All: We give thanks for the cycle of transpiration.

Leader: Water is essential for life. All living things are made up of 70-95% water.

Leader: The earth's surface is covered by 70% water, only 2.5% of this is fresh and 1% is easily available for human use.

Leader: Water is indeed very good; we are thankful.
All: Yes, Water is indeed very good; we are thankful.

Acknowledgment: Many of the words used here are taken from the childrens book, *When Water Lost her Way* by Meg Humphrys. Circles Publishing. 2018. Used with permission. www.circlespublishing.com

Further Possibilities
*A blue cloth placed in the centre of the gathering winding like a river with a bowl of water and a candle placed on it would create a suitable focus and sacred space.
*You may wish to Google 'World Day of Water'.
*Investigate how water is accessible throughout the school. Are there enough water refill stations within the school? Does the canteen sell plastic bottled water and fizzy drinks? If so, what steps can be taken to change this practice?

Community Connection

Community Connection

Celebrating Significant Women in our Lives

Remembering and giving thanks for the significant women in our lives
and for women all over the world.
This ritual could also be used as a broader celebration of Mother's Day or any other time.

Leader: We gather today, giving thanks and expressing gratitude for all the special women in our lives and for women all over the world.

The lit candle acknowledges Divine Presence, in, with and amongst us always.

Make yourself comfortable and become aware of your breathing. Gently notice the air coming in and out.

Leader: Take a moment to think of the many women who are part of your life. As each one comes to mind, imagine them here with you.

Reader 1: We bless all the women in our lives and women all over the world who live in the north.
All: Bless all women who live in the north.

Leader: Take a moment to think of why some of these women are special to you. As each one comes to mind, think of what it is that makes them special.

Reader 2: We bless all the women in our lives and women all over the world who live in the east.
All: Bless all women who live in the east.

Leader: Take a moment to think of what you can do to show these women that you appreciate them in your life.

Reader 3: We bless all the women in our lives and women all over the world who live in the south.
All: Bless all women who live in the south.

Leader: Take a moment and imagine women gathered all over the world. In your mind send them love, courage and gratitude.

Reader 4: We bless all the women in our lives and women all over world who live in the west.
All: Bless all women who live in the west.

Leader: We give thanks for the many ways we notice the presence of God reflected in women all around the world.

All: We give thanks.

Further Possibilities
*Participants invite women significant to them to join in the ritual followed by a shared meal, morning or afternoon tea. Or, alternately, an early morning ritual followed by breakfast.

Celebrating Significant Men in our Lives

Remembering and giving thanks for the significant men in our lives and men throughout the world. This ritual could also be used as a broader celebration of Father's Day or any other time.

Leader: We gather today, giving thanks and expressing gratitude for all the special men in our lives and for men all over the world.

The lit candle reminds us of Divine Presence, in, with and amongst us always.

Pause in silence for a minute. Be sure you are comfortable and become aware of your breathing.

Leader: Take a moment to think of the many men who are part of your life. As each one comes to mind, imagine them here with you.

Reader 1: We bless all the men in our lives and men all over the world who live in the north.
All: We bless all men who live in the north.

Leader: Take a minute to think of why some of these men are special to you. As each one comes to mind, think of what it is that makes them special.

Reader 2: We bless all the men in our lives and men all over the world who live in the east.
All: We bless all men who live in the east.

Leader: Take a minute to think of what you can do show these men that you appreciate them in your life.

Reader 3: We bless all the men in our lives and men all over the world who live in the south.
All: We bless all men who live in the south.

Leader: Take a minute and imagine men gathered all over the world. In your mind, send them love, courage and gratitude.

Reader 4: We bless all the men in our lives and men all over the world who live in the west.
All: We bless all men who live in the west.

Leader: We give thanks for all the ways we notice the presence of Divine Love within all men of the world.

All: We give thanks.

Further Possibilities
*Participants invite men significant to them to join in the ritual followed by a shared meal, morning or afternoon tea. Or, alternately, an early morning ritual followed by breakfast.

Community Connection

Environmental Sabbath - Earth Rest Day
A Litany

The celebration falls on the weekend closest to World Environment Day June 5th; however, this ritual can be celebrated at any other time.

Leader:	We gather for 1 minute in silence as we honour and reverence Mother Earth.
	Pause
Leader:	Blessed be Breath of Life.
All:	Blessed be.
Leader:	Blessed be earth.
All:	Blessed be.
Leader:	Blessed be life cycles that sustain us and all creation.
All:	Blessed be.
Leader:	Blessed be earth, air, fire and water.
All:	Blessed be.
Leader:	Blessed be deserts and seas.
All:	Blessed be.
Leader:	Blessed be flowers, grasses, and trees.
All:	Blessed be.
Leader:	Blessed be produce earth generously provides.
All:	Blessed be.
Leader:	Blessed be those who work towards justice and safe keeping of earth, our common home.
All:	Blessed be.
Leader:	We pause again in silence as we reverence Mother Earth.
	Pause
Leader:	Amen.
All:	Amen.

Further Possibilities
*Participants could add their own spontaneous prayer, 'Blessed be...'
*Participants could create their own litany. The collection of litanies could be copied and bound. These could be used during class prayer and a copy given to other year levels.

Community Connection

National Schools Tree Day

This ritual is best celebrated outside. National Schools Tree Day is an initiative of Planet Ark. Schools Tree Day is traditionally celebrated on the last Friday of July; however, can be celebrated at any time, depending on the ideal time for planting in your region. Gather outside in a circle around a tree in the school grounds, local park, or Botanical Gardens. It would be best if you can name the tree species and gather some interesting facts about it before the ritual.

Leader: We gather in silence around this amazing _____ tree. Sit and simply focus on the tree, its age, colour, shape of the leaves, height, texture of the bark, size of the branches. Notice if there are any birds hovering in the tree.

Pope Francis reminds us that we are not outside nature looking in; we are in nature and nature is in us. [LS:139]

Reader 1: Trees release oxygen when they use energy from sunlight to make glucose from carbon dioxide and water. How amazing. *Pause*

Reader 2: As trees grow, they help stop climate change by removing carbon dioxide from the air, storing carbon in the trees and soil, and releasing oxygen into the atmosphere. How amazing. *Pause*

Reader 3: An average size tree can produce enough oxygen to keep up to 2 or 4 people alive. How amazing. *Pause*

Reader 4: Ecologist Suzanne Simard discovered that trees communicate their needs and send each other nutrients via a network of latticed fungi buried in the soil. How amazing. *Pause*

Reader 5: Trees are the longest living organisms on the planet and one of the earth's greatest natural resources. How amazing. *Pause*

Reader 6: Trees keep our air supply clean, reduce noise pollution, improve water quality, help prevent erosion, provide food and building materials, create shade, provide shelter and homes for creatures, and help make our landscapes look beautiful. How amazing. *Pause*

Reader 7: Many forests around the world are being destroyed. This is called deforestation. Land is being cleared to make it available for other uses, meanwhile damaging our ecology. How tragic. *Pause*

Reader 8: Human-driven deforestation affects wildlife, ecosystems, weather patterns, and even the climate. How tragic. *Pause*

Leader: Pope Francis reminds us of our mutual belonging on earth. [LS:202] In other words, trees belong here just as much as we do. Everything is interdependent. How amazing! *Pause*

Leader: Yes, we commit to plant trees, care for trees, and tell others of their importance to the world's health. Amen.
All: Yes, we commit to plant trees, care for trees, and tell others of their importance to the world's health. Amen.

Further Possibilities
*Explore treedayplanetark.org and you will find a downloadable resource: https://treeday.planetark.org/get-involved/schools
*Students could create signs naming each tree or shrub within the school grounds.
*Research bee and butterfly attracting plants and shrubs. Use some of these for planting.
*Investigate plants indigenous to the area. Create and use signage in an indigenous garden.
*Incorporate a visit to a local park or Botanical Gardens. Often tour guides are available at the Botanical Gardens.
*Participants investigate the amount of oxygen emitted by trees.

NAIDOC Week

NAIDOC Week celebrations are held across Australia each July to celebrate the histories, cultures and achievements of Aboriginal and Torres Strait Islander peoples.

This ritual is best celebrated outside or in another convenient location with the group gathered in a large circle. Incorporation of indigenous artefacts and music would be appropriate.

Leader: We acknowledge the Traditional Custodians of the land on which we gather, the _____ People. (*Add in the name of local Indigenous group.*) We recognise their continuing connection to land and community. We pay respects to Elders past, present and emerging.

Pause

Leader: This week, all of Australia is invited to celebrate the histories, cultures, and achievements of Aboriginal and Torres Strait Islander peoples. We too join in this celebration with an open heart.

As we sit together in silence with open hearts, we know that the land we are on is indeed holy. We know and experience the Great Spirit of Love, in, with and around us.

Reader 1: Aboriginal and Torres Strait Islanders are the First People of Australia.

Reader 2: Australian Aboriginal people are the oldest known civilisation on earth.

Reader 3: Australian Aboriginal people can trace their ancestries back to about 75,000 years ago.

Reader 4: We recognise that we are the same species as First Nations people. We share origins in the great flaring forth, the Divine Spark, at the beginning of creation.

Reader 5: We commit to further connection with First Nations people with whom we share this land Australia.

Leader: Yes, we celebrate the history, culture and achievements of Aboriginal and Torres Strait Islander peoples.
All: We celebrate.

Further Possibilities
*Make connection with local Indigenous artists, story tellers, activists, residents and fellow community members. Invite them to share some of their story, culture, achievements, and hopes and dreams for all people. Be mindful and sensitive of Indigenous students within the school community with inclusion and participation.
*Indigenous music could be woven throughout the ritual.
*Connect with local activities during NAIDOC Week.
*Annual theme and resources available at www.naidoc.org.au
*Posters with the annual theme are available and could be used during the ritual.

Community Connection

National Sorry Day

National Sorry Day is an Australia-wide observance held on May 26th or a nearby day. This marks the beginning of Reconciliation Week. We join voices all over Australia to remember and commit against injustice towards First Nations People and to speak up for Aboriginal Reconciliation.

Leader: We gather in silence remembering First Nations people of Australia. We recognise that we that we are the same species as First Nation people and share origins in the great flaring forth at the beginning of creation.
Pause

Reader 1: We are sorry for the suffering caused to First Nations people of Australia when forcibly removed from their land.
Pause

Reader 2: We are sorry for the disregard given to First Nations people whose families were shattered and separated by the colonisers.
Pause

Reader 3: We are sorry for the long sadness and confusion suffered by the First Nations people.
Pause

Reader 4: A reading from the Gospel of Matthew 22:37-40.
'You shall love God with all your heart and with all your soul, and with all your mind... You shall love your neighbour as you love yourself.' The way we love is what matters.

Reader 5: We recognise the hope and resilience of First Nations people, despite their unimaginable pain when separated from their families and land.

Reader 6: We recognise our own capacity to cause suffering to others in the decisions we make and the words we say.

Reader 7: We recognise the rights of First Nations people and join others to heal the injustice and unfairness that has happened for many years.

Leader: We are committed and enthusiastic for reconciliation and act justly, tenderly and with humility towards all people. Amen.

All: Amen.

Further possibilities
*Each year, a new theme emerges to celebrate National Sorry Day and Reconciliation Week. A simple Google search will find the current year. Resources are available that can be readily incorporated into the ritual and life of the school or community. Planting an indigenous tree and/or plants within the school or community Indigenous garden could be incorporated within the ritual.
*Make connection with local Indigenous artists, story tellers, activists, residents and fellow community members. Invite them to share some of their story, culture, achievements, and hopes and dreams for all people.
*Be mindful and sensitive of Indigenous students within the school community with inclusion and participation.
https://www.reconciliation.org.au/national-reconciliation-week/ 27th May – 3rd June

Community Connection

National Sorry Day: A Lament

National Sorry Day, May 26th, marks the beginning of National Reconciliation Week. Between 1910-1970, many Indigenous children were forcibly removed from their families as a result of various government policies. These children became known as the Stolen Generations. The policies of child removal left a legacy of trauma and loss that continues to affect Indigenous communities, families and individuals.

Leader: We gather on the land where Aboriginal and Torres Strait Islander peoples have walked for over 50,000 years. We pause in respect of First Nations peoples' heritages, cultures and ongoing relationship with land.

Leader: Today, we join many people all over Australia to remember the deep sadness and grief experienced by so many of Australia's First Nations peoples. We particularly acknowledge the continued suffering experienced by Aboriginal people caused by the forcible removable of their children and separation from their families.

Pause for a moment's silence.

Reader 1: We lament the sadness carried by First Nations families who had their children removed by force under the law of the Government.
All: We lament.

Reader 2: We lament the many actions that have taken life, culture, law and language from Australia's First Nations people.
All: We lament.

Reader 3: We lament the continued suffering and dislocation from family of many First Nations people.
All: We lament.

Pause

Reader 4: Jesus said, 'I have come that you may have life and in abundance.' John10:10
Jesus' dream is for everyone.

Leader 5: Let us pause in silence with our hands over hearts, remembering that fullness of life is for all people.

Leader: We commit to being informed, awake and one with First Nations peoples of this continent.
All: We commit.

Further Possibilities
*Each year a new theme emerges to celebrate National Sorry Day and Reconciliation Week. A simple Google search will find the current year. Resources are available that can be readily incorporated into the ritual and life of the school or community.
*Planting an indigenous tree and/or plants within the school or community Indigenous garden could be incorporated within the ritual.

We Remember the World's Refugees with Encouragement, Support and Respect

This ritual can be celebrated during World Refugee Week in June, or other appropriate times.

Leader: Pope Francis reminds us that the world is for all people. He reminds us that all people have a right to be safe, have adequate food and shelter and access to health care. He reminds that we are all sisters and brothers here on planet earth. In caring for earth, we care for all.

Let us sit in silence for a minute as we prepare to remember our sisters and brothers, the world's refugees, with encouragement, support and respect.

Reader 1: We lament the plight of refugees who leave their countries with nothing but hope in their hearts.
All: We lament.

Reader 2: We lament that many people are forced to leave their homelands because of rising sea levels.
All: We lament.

Reader 3: We lament that the majority of refugees are women and children, separated from family.
All: We lament.

Reader 4: We lament that many people lose their lives escaping from their country while hoping for a better life.
All: We lament.

Reader 5: We lament that some governments are unwelcoming to the desperate needs of refugees.
All: We lament.
Pause

Leader: Close your eyes and take a quiet moment to imagine a struggling refugee family and send them your blessing of support and encouragement. *Pause*

Reader 6: We celebrate the strength, determination and hope carried by refugees.
All: We celebrate.

Reader 7: We celebrate the continued contributions and diversity of refugees to their new country.
All: We celebrate.

Reader 8: We celebrate all refugees as sisters and brothers in our one world family.
All: We celebrate.

Leader: In the name of All that Is, we send blessings to refugees of the world. Blessed be refugees.
All: Blessed be refugees.

Further Possibilities
*Be mindful of many students within your setting whose families came to Australia as refugees and others who are in the process of obtaining the necessary documentation to remain here permanently.
*Google your local Refugee Association. Perhaps they can recommend a speaker to share their story.
*Google World Refugee Week for the current theme plus many resources and ideas.
*Many students will be familiar with Ahn Do, and his books telling of his journey from Vietnam to Australia. The Luckiest Refugee by Ahn Do and The Little Refugee written by Ahn Do and Suzanne Do. These books could be used during Refugee week and as a lead up to the ritual.

Liturgical Moments

Lent: A Time to Reflect on the Way We are Living our Lives

This ritual can be celebrated each week during Lent.
The 40 days of Lent are a time of reflection and preparation leading towards the great feast of Easter. The ashes on our forehead on Ash Wednesday remind us that we are made of Star Dust from the primal outpouring, billions of years ago. Yes, the outpouring of Divine Love!

Leader: Lent, following Ash Wednesday, is like an opportunity for a spiritual make over. We are given the chance to reflect on how we are living our lives as we move towards the great celebration of Easter.

Leader: We are invited to be patient with ourselves and others, knowing that we can start all over again every day.

Leader: As we gather in silence, be mindful of your breathing. Notice when the in breath becomes the out breath and when the out breath becomes the in breath.

Leader: Think about the things you do and say. Are they building up or breaking down the active presence of Divine Love in your relationships, with yourselves, others, the environment and the wider world? *Pause*

Leader: Think about the things you do and say. Are they building up or breaking down the active presence of Divine Love in bringing forth justice, compassion and inclusion? *Pause*

Leader: Think about the things you do and say. Are they building up or breaking down the active presence of Divine Love in your care for the earth, your protection of all creatures and your responsible use of goods? *Pause*

Reader 1: During Lent, I let go of putdowns and take up encouraging others.
All: During Lent, I encourage others.

Pause

Reader 2: During Lent, I let go of blame and take up personal responsibility.
All: During Lent, I am personally responsible.

Pause

Reader 3: During Lent, I let go of wasting food and materials and take up using only what I need.
All: During Lent, I use only what I need.

Pause

Leader: As we conclude, we are mindful of our commitment to do some things differently. We acknowledge Divine Love is in, with and around us.

All: Amen.

Further Possibilities
*The ritual can be celebrated each week during Lent. Participants spontaneously create their own phrase. 'During Lent, I let go of...' 'During Lent, I ...'
*Participant could use their journals when responding to the reflective questions.

Liturgical Moments

Celebrating the Hope of Easter

This ritual can be celebrated at Easter or other suitable time.

Leader: Today, we come together and give thanks for Jesus, a sign of great love and hope for all people.

Reader 1: We light this candle. We acknowledge the presence of Divine Mystery in, with, and around us and all of creation.

Leader: As we gather in silence, become aware of your breathing. Notice the flickering candle. Its colour and movement.

Leader: Today, we celebrate the great mystery of Easter and give thanks for Jesus and the hope he shared with those around him.

Reader 2: We give thanks for Jesus who opened his heart to the greatest mystery of all, Divine Love.

Reader 3: We give thank for Jesus who lived passionately, believing Divine Love in, with, and around all people and all of creation.

Reader 4: We give thanks for Jesus who trusted the presence of Divine Love, even when things became tough for him.

Right Side: We notice the action of Divine Love when we spend time with our friends.
All: We notice.

Left Side: We notice the action of Divine Love when we listen to the sounds of nature.
All: We notice.

Right Side: We notice the action of Divine Love when people speak out against injustice.
All: We notice.

Left Side: We notice the action of Divine Love when we are welcomed and understood.
All: We notice.

Right Side: We notice the action of Divine Love when we work actively to care for earth.
All: We notice.

Invitation for spontaneous responses. 'We notice Divine Love when...

Leader: As we leave today, we commit to noticing Divine Love in action.
All: We commit to noticing Divine Love in action.

Further Possibilities
*Have a container of glass beads in the centre near the candle. Invite participants to add their own response. 'We notice Divine Love when...' After each one speaks, a glass bead is placed around the candle.
*Participants follow up by gathering various images and photos. They create a banner for each image. 'Divine Love in Action.'

© 'Sparks of the Universe' Jennifer Callanan

Liturgical Moments

Creator Spirit: Ever Present

This ritual can be celebrated around Pentecost, at the beginning of class meeting, SRC meeting or other moments of gathering.

Leader: We gather in silence, just as Mary did with the disciples on the day of Pentecost.

Become aware of your breath. Feel the air coming in and out of your body, filling your lungs and releasing.

Reader 1: We celebrate the presence of Creator Spirit within everyone and everything.
All: We celebrate.

Reader 2: We celebrate Jesus, aware of Creator Spirit within himself, his experiences and all creation.
All: We celebrate.

Reader 3: We celebrate Creator Spirit in our daily acts of compassion, friendship and courage.
All: We celebrate.

Reader 4: We celebrate Creator Spirit in strong wind, in gentle rain, roaring fire, and in flowing water.
All: We celebrate.

Reader 5: We celebrate that, like Jesus, we too are awake to Creator Spirit in, with, and around us.
All: We celebrate.

Leader: We celebrate Creator Spirit.
All: We celebrate Creator Spirit.

Further Possibilities
Gather outside and celebrate the ritual around a fire pit. Prior to the ritual, invite participants to sit in silence focusing on the colour, movement and warmth of the fire.

Liturgical Moments

Love is Born

This ritual focuses on the feast of Christmas; however, it can be used at any time.

Leader: We gather together knowing that very soon we will celebrate the great feast of Christmas. We join many people all around the world remembering and celebrating the birth of Jesus.

As you sit, focus your eyes on the candle in the centre. Become still and quiet.

Reader 1: We light this candle, acknowledging the Light of Love reflected in Jesus and within each of us.

Reader 2: Today we join many people around the world remembering and celebrating the birth of Jesus.

Reader 3: As Jesus grew, he became aware of God's Spirit of Love, in him, with him and around him, in all of creation and every human being. Yes, and that includes each of us!

Reader 4: Jesus shared his deep experience of God's Spirit of Love with others through the everyday actions of his life.

Reader 5: Jesus grew to know that God's dream of Love was for all people to be happy, treated fairly, shown compassion, and to know deeply that they are loved with a never-ending love.

Reader 6: Jesus taught us that love is born through our everyday actions.

Side 1: Love is born when we show kindness and care to others and creation in very real ways.
All: Love is born.

Side 2: Love is born when forgiveness, inclusion, justice and truth are present.
All: Love is born.

Side 1: Love is born when we are aware of our connection with all of creation.
All: Love is born.

Side 2: Love is born when a flower blooms, a bird sings, a star sparkles.
All: Love is born.

Side 1: Love is born when we least expect it.
All: Love is born.

Pause

Leader: Yes, Love is born.
All: Yes, Love is born.

Response inspired by Michael Leunig's verse, 'Love is Born'.

Further Possibilities
*Gather a variety of images depicting the nativity scene and place these around the centre candle.
*Students compare the birth of Jesus from Luke 2:1-20 and Matthew 1:18-25.
*Younger students enact one of the stories of the Birth of Jesus.
*Students create their own litany 'Love is Born' and create a book shared with other classes.
*Images are collected showing the many ways love is born. Participants place images around the candle after each prayer.

Noticing the Seasons

Noticing Autumn

Leader: As we pause to celebrate and give thanks for the season of autumn, let us become still. Notice your breathing. In and out. Become aware when the in breath becomes the out breath and when the out breath becomes the in breath.

Reader 1: Many trees lose their leaves in autumn. Various colours fall to the ground. In time, leaves become crisp and return to the earth.
Blessed be the colours of autumn.
All: Blessed be the colours of autumn.

Reader 2: Various fruits and vegetables are ripe and ready for eating in autumn.
Blessed be the produce of autumn.
All: Blessed be the produce of autumn.

Reader 3: The days gradually become shorter and the nights become cooler in autumn.
Blessed be the changes of autumn.
All: Blessed be the changes of autumn.

Reader 4: Many birds migrate to warmer climates where they can find food and shelter in autumn.
Blessed be bird migration in autumn.
All: Blessed be bird migration in autumn.

Reader 5: Trees, vegetables, and bulbs are planted in the warm soil knowing the nourishing winter rain is on its way.
Blessed be the planting cycle.
All: Blessed be the planting cycle.

Invitation for participants to add their own phrase and response.

Reader 6: If Earth was not tilted on its axis, there would be no seasons, and humanity would suffer. When a Mars-size object collided with Earth 4.5 billion years ago, it knocked off a chunk that would become the moon. It also tilted Earth sideways a bit, so that our planet now orbits the sun on a slant. How amazing.

Leader: Blessed be the gifts of autumn.
All: Blessed be the gifts of autumn.

Further Possibilities:
*Participants could later create their own autumn ritual using the model above and use it when leading class prayer or other occasions.
*Become aware of seasonal fruits and vegetables. At the beginning of autumn, list the fruits and vegetables that grow locally, at this time. Invite students to bring a piece of seasonal fruit or vegetable for simple sharing, soup making, etc. Emphasise freshness of local produce, carbon impact on transported produce, and implications of storage on out of season produce.
*A collection of various autumn leaves could be used to create an outdoor nature mandala. The mandala could then be used to gather around in silence, appreciating the beauty of the changing season.

Noticing the Seasons

Autumn Equinox

An equinox occurs when the position of the sun is exactly over the equator. The autumnal equinox occurs around March 21st in the Southern Hemisphere and around September 23rd in the Northern Hemisphere.

Leader: Today, we celebrate the extraordinary moment when both the north and south poles are equal distance from the sun. We celebrate the Autumn Equinox.

Become aware of your breathing as you come to stillness.

Reader 1: We light the centre candle reminding us of the extraordinary presence of Creative Divine Love, in, with and around us and every spark of the universe.

Reader 2: For a single moment, twice a year, day and night are roughly equal in the Northern and Southern Hemisphere on the date of the equinox.
Left Side: How extraordinary.

Reader 3: At the Autumn Equinox, we celebrate the beginning of Autumn and movement towards the winter solstice, the longest night and shortest day.
Right Side: How extraordinary.

Reader 4: At the equinoxes, the sun appears overhead at noon as seen from Earth's equator.
Left Side: How extraordinary.

Reader 5: The sun rises due east and sets due west for all of us on the day of an equinox.
Right Side: How extraordinary.

Reader 6: After the Autumn Equinox, we notice colour, beauty and change preparing for an end and eventually a new beginning.
Left Side: How extraordinary.

Leader: We give thanks for Brother Sun, bringing us day and light; and shining with strength and magnificence.

(Line adapted from *Canticle of Creation*, St Francis of Assisi)

All: We give thanks for Brother Sun at this time of Autumn Equinox.

Further Possibilities
*Place a globe of the earth in the centre of the circle and another sphere representing the sun.
*Prior to the ritual, participants investigate why the sun rises due east and sets due west for us all except for the north and south pole, at the time of the equinox.
*Prior to the ritual, participants research the difference between solstice and equinox.
*Take participants outside at midday to notice the position of the sun.
*Invite participants to go outside around sunrise or sunset and notice the location of the sun on the horizon. At sunrise, this point will be due east; at sunset, this point will be due west.
*Participants research customs around the world at the time of the Autumn Equinox.

An Autumn Meditation: Creating a Mandala

The autumn mandala can be created within the school grounds, on camp, during retreat, in the local parklands, wherever there is an abundance of autumn leaves that have fallen to the ground. Mandalas are a form of meditation.

Gather in a large circle with a candle or other item indicating the centre of the circle.

Leader: We stand together in this circle, with no beginning and no end.
We honour the natural beauty and diversity of colour during the changes of Autumn.

With your eyes open, feel your feet on the ground. Notice the grass and leaves around you.

Become aware of the beginning, middle and end of each breath. Notice the air entering and leaving your body.

Leader: Today we will create an Autumn mandala using the fallen leaves around us. In silence we will gather leaves and place them around the candle, slowly creating a circle of colour. As we wander around gathering and placing leaves, we are mindful of the colourful reflection of Divine Love.

Allow plenty of time for the circle to be completely filled with the autumn leaves.

At the completion, gather the group around the mandala in silence.

Right side: Divine Love is present in the diversity of colour.

Left side: Divine Love is present in various shapes.

Right side: Divine Love is present in creativity within each of us.

Left Side: Divine Love is present.
Pause

Leader: We will leave our mandala now to eventually decompose and return to the earth.

Further Possibilities
Participants gather in small groups and together create a mandala. At the conclusion, participants wander around in silence appreciating the many mandalas created by their friends and colleagues.

Noticing Winter

Leader: As we pause to celebrate and give thanks for the season of winter, let us become still. Notice your breathing, gently, in and out. Become aware when the in breath becomes the out breath and when the out breath becomes the in breath.

Pause

Reader 1: In winter Divine Presence is active when flowers, trees, and grasses appear to be resting. In winter, Life is present.
All: In winter, Life is present!

Reader 2: In winter, Divine Presence is active through grey clouds, rain, snow, hailstones, gusty wind, and extreme cold. In winter Life is active.
All: In winter, Life is active.

Reader 3: In winter, we imagine the earth and plants delighting in heavy rains, running streams and nurturing life. In winter we imagine.
All: In winter, we imagine.

Reader 4: In winter, we experience shorter days, dark clouds, warm clothing and nourishing hot food.
All: In winter, we experience.

Invitation for participants to add their own phrase and response.

Reader 5: If Earth was not tilted on its axis, there would be no seasons, and humanity would suffer. When a Mars-size object collided with Earth 4.5 billion years ago, it knocked off a chunk that would become the moon. It also tilted Earth sideways a bit, so that our planet now orbits the sun on a slant. How amazing.

Reader 6: In winter, Divine Presence prepares for new possibilities.
All: In winter, Divine Presence prepares.

Leader: Blessed be winter.
All: Blessed be winter.

Further Possibilities
*Participants could later create their own winter ritual using the model above and use it when leading class prayer or other occasions.
*Becoming aware of seasonal fruits and vegetables. At the beginning of winter, list the fruits and vegetables that grow locally, at this time. Invite students to bring a piece of seasonal fruit or vegetable for simple sharing, soup making, etc. Emphasise freshness of local produce, carbon impact on transported produce, and implications of storage on out of season produce.

Noticing the Seasons

Winter Solstice

Leader: Today, we gather to celebrate the Winter Solstice.

The Winter Solstice occurs once a year and in the Southern Hemisphere can fall on June 21st, 22nd or 23rd. This day has the least daylight hours. At the same time, the Summer Solstice occurs in the Northern Hemisphere where the day has the most daylight hours.

Leader: As we stand together in a circle, become aware of the ground under your feet and notice your breathing.

Today, we gather to celebrate the Winter Solstice

As we light the candle, we reverence the presence of Divine Mystery in our unfolding universe.

The candle is lit.

Reader 1: We cannot feel it. However, we know that earth is rotating and revolving around the sun.
Pause

Reader 2: We are mindful that in the rotation, the position of earth determines the timing of day and night in each hemisphere.
Pause

Reader 3: We are grateful for the light and heat constantly radiating towards earth.
Pause

Reader 4: We are aware that today has the least daylight hours of all days of the year.
Pause

Reader 5: We are conscious that, after today, the daylight hours slowly begin to increase.
Pause

Leader: Today, we are mindful that we have solstices and seasons, because Earth is tilted on its axis about 23.5 degrees. This causes each hemisphere to receive different amounts of sunlight throughout the year.

We give thanks for the gift of our extraordinary, unfolding universe.

All: We give thanks for the gift of our extraordinary, unfolding universe.

Further Possibilities
*Encourage the group to chart the sunrise and sunset hours the week before and after the Winter Solstice.
*Research the latest sunrise day and time and the latest sunset day and time. Notice that they don't occur on the same day! We can thank earth's tilt and our elliptical orbit around the sun for this astronomical quirk!

Noticing Spring

Leader: As we pause to celebrate and give thanks for the season of spring, let us become still. Notice your breathing. In and out. Become aware when the in breath becomes the out breath and when the out breath becomes the in breath.

Reader 1: In spring, the plants stir from their apparent quiet activity during winter.
In spring, we notice plants stirring.
All: In spring, we notice plants stirring.

Reader 2: In spring, daylight begins to lengthen, green growth begins to appear, and buds begin to form.
In spring, we notice new growth.
All: In spring, we notice new growth.

Reader 3: In spring, wildflowers, daffodils and other colourful surprises become present.
In spring, we delight in noticing emerging colours.
All: In spring, we delight in noticing emerging colours.

Reader 4: In spring, new life and possibilities come forth in surprising ways.
In spring, we notice new possibilities.
All: In spring, we notice new possibilities.

Invitation for participants to add their own phrase and response.

Reader 5: If Earth was not tilted on its axis, there would be no seasons, and humanity would suffer. When a Mars-size object collided with Earth 4.5 billion years ago, it knocked off a chunk that would become the moon. It also tilted Earth sideways a bit, so that our planet now orbits the sun on a slant. How amazing.

Reader 6: In spring, Creator Spirit is present in a variety of colours.
In spring, Creator Spirit is present.
All: In spring, Creator Spirit is present.

Leader: Blessed be spring.
All: Blessed be spring.

Further Possibilities
*Participants could later create their own spring ritual using the model above and use it when leading class prayer or other occasions.
*Become aware of seasonal fruits and vegetables. At the beginning of spring, list the fruits and vegetables that grow locally, at this time. Invite students to bring a piece of seasonal fruit or vegetable for simple sharing, soup making, etc. Emphasise freshness of local produce, carbon impact on transported produce, and implications of storage on out of season produce.

Spring Equinox

An equinox occurs when the position of the sun is exactly over the equator. The spring equinox occurs around September 23rd in the Southern Hemisphere and around March 21st in the Northern Hemisphere.

Leader: Today, we celebrate the extraordinary moment when both the north and south poles are equal distance from the sun. We celebrate the Spring Equinox.

Become aware of your breathing as you come to stillness.

Reader 1: We light the centre candle, reminding us of the extraordinary presence of Creative Divine Love, in, with and around us and every spark of the universe.

Reader 2: For a single moment, twice a year, day and night are roughly equal in the Northern and Southern Hemisphere on the date of the equinox.
Left Side: How extraordinary.

Reader 3: At the Spring Equinox, we celebrate the beginning of Spring and movement towards the summer solstice, the shortest night and longest day.
Right Side: How extraordinary.

Reader 4: At the equinoxes, the sun appears overhead at noon as seen from Earth's equator.
Left Side: How extraordinary.

Reader 5: The sun rises due east and sets due west for all of us on the day of an equinox.
Right Side: How extraordinary.

Reader 6: After the Spring Equinox, we notice new light and life, new beginnings and possibilities.
Left Side: How extraordinary.

Leader: We give thanks for Brother Sun, bringing us day and light; and shining with strength and magnificence.
(Line adapted from Canticle of Creation, St Francis of Assisi)

All: We give thanks for Brother Sun at this time of Spring Equinox.

Further Possibilities
*Place a globe of the earth in the centre of the circle and another sphere representing the sun.
*Prior to the ritual, participants investigate why the sun rises due east and sets due west for us all except for the north and south pole, at the time of the equinox.
*Prior to the ritual, participants research the difference between solstice and equinox.
*Take participants outside at midday to notice the position of the sun.
*Invite participants to go outside around sunrise or sunset and notice the location of the sun on the horizon. At sunrise, this point will be due east; at sunset, this point will be due west.
*Participants research customs around the world at the time of the Spring Equinox.

Noticing Summer

Leader: As we pause to celebrate and give thanks for the season of summer, let us become still. Notice your breathing. In and out. Become aware when the in breath becomes the out breath and when the out breath becomes the in breath.

Reader 1: In summer, days become warmer and the sun shines longer.
All: We notice warmth and wear lighter clothing.

Reader 2: In summer, the land is dry and in need of water.
All: We see dry and brown paddocks.

Reader 3: In summer, the garden begins to produce varieties of vegetables and fruits.
All: We experience a range of delicious tastes.

Reader 4: In summer, the power of fire is sometimes present.
All: We are aware of the unpredictability of mother nature.

Reader 5: In summer, we cool down in rivers, pools and the sea.
All: We are grateful for and mindful of refreshing water.

Invitation for participants to add their own phrase and response.

Reader 6: If Earth was not tilted on its axis, there would be no seasons, and humanity would suffer. When a Mars-size object collided with Earth 4.5 billion years ago, it knocked off a chunk that would become the moon. It also tilted Earth sideways a bit, so that our planet now orbits the sun on a slant. How amazing.

Leader: Blessed be summer.
All: Blessed be summer.

Further Possibilities
*Participants could later create their own summer ritual using the model above and use it when leading class prayer or other occasions.
*Become aware of seasonal fruits and vegetables. At the beginning of summer, list the fruits and vegetables that grow locally, at this time. Invite students to bring a piece of seasonal fruit or vegetable for simple sharing, soup making, etc. Emphasise freshness of local produce, carbon impact on transported produce, and implications of storage on out of season produce.

Summer Solstice

Leader: Today, we gather to celebrate the Summer Solstice.

The Summer Solstice occurs once a year and in the Southern Hemisphere can fall on December 20th, 21st, 22nd or 23rd. This day has the most daylight hours. At the same time, the Winter Solstice occurs in the Northern Hemisphere where the day has the least daylight hours.

Leader: As we stand together in a circle, become aware of the ground under your feet and notice your breathing.

As we light the candle, we reverence the presence of Divine Mystery in our unfolding universe.

The candle is lit.

Reader 1: We cannot feel it. However, we know that earth is rotating and revolving around the sun.
Pause

Reader 2: We are mindful that in the rotation, the position of earth determines the timing of day and night in each hemisphere.
Pause

Reader 3: We are grateful for the light and heat constantly radiating towards earth.
Pause

Reader 4: We are aware that today has the most daylight hours of all days of the year.
Pause

Reader 5: We are conscious that, after today, the day light hours slowly begin to shorten.
Pause

Leader: Today, we are mindful that we have solstices and seasons, because Earth is tilted on its axis about 23.5 degrees. This causes each hemisphere to receive different amounts of sunlight throughout the year.

We give thanks for the gift of our extraordinary, unfolding universe.

All: We give thanks for the gift of our extraordinary, unfolding universe.

Further Possibilities
*Encourage the group to chart the sunrise and sunset hours the week before and after Summer Solstice.
*Research the earliest sunrise day and time and the earliest sunset day and time. Notice that they don't occur on the same day! We can thank Earth's tilt and our elliptical orbit around the sun for this astronomical quirk!

Seasonal Fruits and Vegetables: Sparking the Imagination

This ritual could be celebrated midway through each of the seasons.
Prior the ritual, participants are invited to bring seasonal fruits and vegetables for sharing.
The fruit and vegetables are cut into bite-size pieces and placed on serving platters.

Leader: We are mindful of the abundance of produce grown that forms our daily diet, nourishes our growth and excites our taste buds. Today, we will enjoy gifts from Mother Earth, seasonal fruits and vegetables; and take time to appreciate each bite!

The platters are placed in the centre of the gathered circle.

As we pause in silence, become aware of your breathing, in and out, in and out.

The candle is lit.

Reader:	Great Mystery is present amid seasonal fruits and vegetables.
All:	Great Mystery is present amid seasonal fruits and vegetables.
Leader:	I invite you to raise your right hand in a gesture of blessing towards the fruit and vegetables.
Leader:	We bless this abundant produce from Mother Earth.
All:	We bless this abundant produce from Mother Earth.
Leader:	We are grateful.
All:	We are grateful.

Leader: As you focus on the produce in the centre, imagine the person or persons who have grown these fruits and vegetables. Imagine how they prepared the soil, ensured adequate water, pruned if necessary, added nourishment, protected it from wind and harsh conditions, checked each stage of growth, and prepared it for harvesting, packaging and sale.

Leader: Now become aware of the soil, a mixture of organic matter, minerals, gases, liquids, and organisms that together supported the growth of the fruits and vegetables. We now imagine the bees whose work of pollination is essential for fruits and vegetables to grow.

Leader: As I pass the platter of fruit and vegetables around, take one piece and eat it in silence. Notice the feeling on your tongue, the taste and texture.

Pass the platter around several times.

Leader: We are grateful for produce from Mother Earth.
All: We are grateful for produce from Mother Earth.

Further Possibilities
*Students choose a piece of fruit or vegetable and track the process from grower to consumer. They note where it is grown, conditions required for growth, the growing cycle, distance it has travelled to be available locally, the carbon footprint created, the origins of the species and derivations, how it can be used in cooking and grown at home, actual cost of production and any further information.

Bibliography and Resources

Attenborough, D. Cited in *The Ecologist - The Journal for the Post-Industrial Age.* 4th April 2013 in article by Matt Adam Williams 'Securing Nature's Future.' [Internet]. Available from: https://theecologist.org/2013/apr/04/securing-natures-future [Accessed 15 August 2019].

Berry, T. *It Takes a Universe* [Internet] Available from:http://thomasberry.org/publications-and-media/it-takes-a-universe [Accessed 1 August 2019]

Berry, T. (1999). *The Great Work: Our Way into the Future.* Harmony/Bell New York: Tower, p. 81.

Catholic Church (1992) *Catechism of the Catholic Church.* [Internet].Vatican City: Libreria Editrice Vaticana. Available from: http://www.vatican.va/archive/ENG0015/___P24.HTM [Accessed 12 November 2018]

Catholic Earth Care Australia http://catholicearthcare.org.au/
Note: Vision for Earth Care Australia is for an ecological sustainable and resilient Australia, where Catholic Communities play an active part in the holistic care of social, human and environment ecology. They provide a number of resources to schools, parishes and community organisations to assist in their sustainability journey.

Cool Australia https://www.coolaustralia.org/Mission: To help foster the next generation of change makers to ensure a sustainable future.
Note: Resources for Students, Educators and Professional Development are available.

Cox, B. [Internet] Available from: https://www.azquotes.com/author/19446-Brian_Cox [Accessed 7-3-2019]

Darnel, T. *How the Universe was Formed* 3.27mins YouTube DeepAstronomy.com https://www.youtube.com/watch?v=s43lkwCsPPg

Deep Time Walk Free App https://www.deeptimewalk.org/
Note: The Deep Time Walk calculates your speed and distance as you journey across 4.6bn years of time, enabling you to learn about key evolutionary events as they occur and comprehend the destructive impact of humans on the Earth's complex climate.

Earth Hour https://www.earthhour.org.au

Earth compared to the rest of the Universe: Amazing Graphic Presentation.
https://www.youtube.com/watch?v=1Eh5BpSnBBw

Extinction Rebellion. Australian Website https://ausrebellion.earth/
Note: A focus on stopping the 6th mass extinction.

Generation Waking Up http://www.bethechange.org.au/programs/generation-waking-up/
Note: Generation Waking Up is a global campaign to ignite a generation of young people to bring forth a thriving, just and sustainable world.

Global Catholic Climate Movement https://catholicclimatemovement.global/

How the Universe was Formed
https://www.youtube.com/watch?v=s43lkwCsPPg

How Whales Change Climate
YouTube: https://www.youtube.com/watch?v=M18HxXve3CM#action=share

Humphrys. M. (2018) *When Water Lost her Way* Circles Publishing, Cowes, Victoria. www.circlespublishing.com

Kearney, P. http://www.peterkearneysongs.com.au/

Kearney, P. (1996) *All the World is Sacred* [CD ROM] Crossover Music. NSW https://store.cdbaby.com/cd/peterkearney5

Laudato Si', Animation for Children. Catholic Agency for Overseas Development. United Kingdom. https://cafod.org.uk/Education/Primary-teaching-resources/Laudato-Si-animation [Accessed 5-8-2019]

Leunig, M. *Love is Born* https://www.leunig.com.au [Accessed 3 July 2019]

Martin, W. D. (2018) *Mother I Feel You* Track11, CD titled, 'Love is the Medicine' Downloadable from website: http://www.windsongmakani.com/

NAIDOC Week https://www.naidoc.org.au/
National Reconciliation Week https://www.reconciliation.org.au/national-reconciliation-week/

National Tree Day https://treeday.planetark.org/get-involved/schools

NRM: Natural Resource Management http://nrmregionsaustralia.com.au/

Pope Francis, (2015) *Encyclical Letter Laudato Si' On Care for our Common Home.* St Pauls Publications. Strathfield, NSW.

Refugee Week https://www.refugeeweek.org.au/

Richards, C. (2019) *The Healing Power of the Whales' Song.* [Internet] Available from: https://upliftconnect.com/healing-power-whales-song/ [Accessed 14 May 2019] For Further Information go to www.chiprichards.global

SkyView Lite Free App - Exploring the Universe. When the App is open and tablet or phone is facing the night sky, names of stars, planets and constellations appear on the screen.

Stargazing Live ABC Series Available from:
https://www.abc.net.au/tv/programs/stargazing-live/ [Accessed 21 May 2019]
Note: Broadcast over three nights from Siding Spring Observatory in NSW, the series immerses audiences in a celebration of the night sky, with a focus on features that are best experienced from Australian soil.

Sustainable Human https://www.sustainablehuman.com
Note: Sustainable Human is a website creating and sharing stories that offer an interconnected view of the world. There is an abundance of resources available here.

The Cosmic Walk [Internet]. Available from http://monmouthpresbytery.com/wp-content/uploads/pre2016-files/Genesis-Farm-Cosmic-Walk.pdf [Accessed 26 April 2019]

The Great Story Website: http://www.thegreatstory.org/home.html
Note: Contains an abundance of resources and information: Big History; Epic of Evolution; Inspiring Naturalism.

The Nature Conservancy Australia. [Internet] Available from: https://www.natureaustralia.org.au/explore/australian-animals/australia-s-endangered-animals/[Accessed 14 January 2019]

Thunberg, G. (2019) https://www.theguardian.com/world/2019/mar/11/greta-thunberg-schoolgirl-climate-change-warrior-some-people-can-let-things-go-i-cant [Accessed 2 April 2019].

Thunberg, G. (2018) *Address to the United Nations Negotiators and Climate Activists* Poland 17-12-2018 [Internet] Available from: https://climatesafety.info/meet-2018s-climate-oracle/ [Accessed 23 February 2019]

War on Waste. [Internet] ABC Series. Available from: https://www.abc.net.au/ourfocus/waronwaste/ [Accessed 3 May 2019]
Note: ABC series with Craig Reucassel, on a mission to see if we, as a nation, can reduce our waste. The website includes various resources that could be used with Upper Primary and Secondary Students. There is an action tool kit that could be used as a model and adapted for your setting.

2040 This movie explores what the future could look like by the year 2040 if we embraced the best solutions already available to us to improve the planet. Director and Writer Damon Gameau. Further information including resources for use available here: http://www.whatsyour2040.com/

50 Fascinating Facts about the Ocean [Internet] Available from: https://www.divein.com/articles/ocean-facts/ [Accessed 10 December 2018]

www.ingramcontent.com/pod-product-compliance
Lightning Source LLC
Chambersburg PA
CBHW080857010526
44107CB00058B/2601